A Welsh Childhood

A Welsh Childhood

ALICE THOMAS ELLIS

Photographs by Patrick Sutherland

A COMMON READER EDITION

MOYER BELL
Wakefield, Rhode Island & London

A Welsh Childhood

A COMMON READER EDITION
Published by The Akadine Press / Moyer Bell

Text copyright © 1990, 1997 by Alice Thomas Ellis
Photographs copyright © 1990, 1997 by Patrick Sutherland
First published in the United Kingdom by Michael Joseph Ltd., 1990

A COMMON READER EDITION and fountain colophon are trademarks of The Akadine Press, Inc.

**LIBRARY OF CONGRESS
CATALOGING-IN-PUBLICATION DATA**

Ellis, Alice Thomas.
 A Welsh Childhood / Alice Thomas Ellis: photographs by Patrick Sutherland—1st edition.

 p.   cm.
 Originally published by London: Michael Joseph, 1990
 1. Ellis, Alice Thomas—Childhood and youth. 2. Women Novelists, Welsh—20th Century—
Biography. 3. Wales, North—Social Life and customs. I. Sutherland, Patrick. II Title
 PR6055.L4856Z464   2000
 823'.914—dc20   96-31234
 ISBN 1-55921-283-7 (pb)   CIP

Printed in China by Palace Press International.
Distributed in North America by Publishers Group West, 1700 Fourth Street,
Berkeley CA 94710, 800-788-3123 (in California 510-528-1444);
and in Europe by Gazelle Book Services Ltd., Falcon House, Queen Square,
Lancaster LA1 1RN England 524-68765.

To Kyffin Williams with love

I WAS BROUGHT up in a place called Penmaenmawr which, literally translated, means rather unbeautifully Big Rock Head. It lies between Conwy and Bangor on the North Wales coast. We thought of it as a village, but rich Edwardians from Liverpool and Manchester, cotton merchants and shipowners, had seen it as a watering-place and had built large hotels and villas of varying sizes on its slopes: they had laid out a golf course, gardens and tennis courts, planted a few palms, monkey

puzzles and exotic grasses, and rendered it genteel. Five minutes' walk from the last of the villas would bring you to the first of the hill-farms where life went on in the old way, so the place had a slightly schizoid air. I think of a person, showing a bit of midriff, wearing a silk skirt and, above it, a worn and practical flannel shirt. Add to this the fact that as you walk a little way from the first of the hill-farms you come to a granite quarry banging and blasting away, and you have a place the precise ambience of which is difficult to describe.

Going a mile or so downhill, once upon a time you would have come to a broad and peaceful coastline: a promenade, beach huts and the long and level sands. That's all gone. The sea is still there, naturally enough, but the Welsh Office is throwing a road all round the coast and, while at the moment the end result is difficult to foresee, I doubt whether ever again anyone will paddle out there with any pleasure. I will return later to the subject of this road, but at present I am remembering Pen – as it was always known for short – as it used to be: *my* Pen, that is, for every inhabitant, every visitor sees a place differently, and I don't suppose the Pen of the farmers, the quarrymen, the women who belonged to the Band of Hope, the golfers, the trippers would resemble mine at all closely.

To begin with, when I was small, I saw only its smallest aspects. The convolvulus growing round the advert for Brylcreem on the station platform, the gull on the railway bridge, the drain in the gutter outside the station where, one day, my mother lost her sunglasses. I seldom looked up at the hills, because I have never much cared for panoramic views and vast sights unless something unusual or interesting is happening to them at the time – a spectacular sunset or a thunderstorm. I like to know they're there, you understand – not being bulldozed for the benefit of the traffic or subjected to death by conifer – but I never spent much time contemplating them. I have the same feeling about mothers. You don't want to sit on their lap all the time while they comb your curls, but you like to know they're around, going on in the usual fashion without being raped or murdered.

My mother, a Griffiths, had been born in Cardiff, but the family had moved to Liverpool – known then as the capital of North Wales – and she had married my father who was of Russo-Finnish descent. Liverpool was a great melting pot. I was born there. My father had spent all his holidays in North Wales, fishing and shooting with *his* father, who had retired from the sea and owned a pub – The Nook in Nelson Street – until, for some reason never understood, he had shot himself. Most of my mother's relations still lived in Wales, several of them having moved from the South to Caernarvonshire, and married local people. This was fortunate since it made it inevitable that we should continue to spend most of our time in Wales.

One of my earliest memories is of picnicking very early one morning by the edge of a cornfield bright with poppies, sitting on the running board of the car and eating hard-boiled eggs, asking how long it would be before we saw the sea. I have never felt truly at ease or at home anywhere but in Wales. I fell in love with the land as I believe people are supposed to fall in love with other people. I wanted to be one flesh with it. To this end I have already arranged for my place of burial.

WE USED TO stay with my cousin Primrose who had married a farmer's son and lived in a house on the coast road, as it was then. Its garden, like all the gardens in Penmaenmawr, fell down towards the sea. It was in that garden that I first started to learn about death: not bereavement, just death. We would go, each morning, to the beach where we would eat sandwiches with sand in them – there used to be a large metal hen on the promenade: you put money in it and it laid a tin egg containing a present – and then, in case I should get sunstroke or over-excited, we would return so that I could play in the garden within safe reach of the house, and I always brought back a bucketful of shrimps and tiny crabs, and they always died before bedtime.

That garden was always littered with dead birds too. Either there was an unusually lethal bunch of cats around or it was another of those Welsh places where birds cannot fly without dropping dead. The steep slope was covered with harsh, sea-stained grass; the only flowers that would grow were fuchsia and valerian (which are my least favoured of all blooms) and the occasional lupin. It sounds, as I describe it, an unpleasant place, but I spent many hours there, close to the ground, eyeball to eyeball with the ants and caterpillars, laying out ground-plans for houses with the pebbles that had also come home in the bucket.

I don't remember much about the people at that time, since even when I stood up I could see scarcely higher than their knees, and we had very little in common. I took them for granted, being – not spoiled, for my mother was rather strict – but unexceptionably well cared for. I remember some of my clothes better: a woollen bathing costume with a diving lady appliquéd on to it, which was of very little use to me since I resolutely refused to go into the sea above my ankles. I had once tried total immersion and hadn't liked it (in fact I had once slipped off the jetty and nearly drowned), so in this way I was a disappointment to my family. Then I had a dark blue frock with a matching bolero with flowers embroidered on it, a brown knitted frock with a flared skirt and a yellow mackintosh and sou'wester. My other frocks were mostly made of gingham, buttoned through with Peter Pan collars and rather boring. Still, I did have an angora cardigan which I recall as very chic, although the fluff made me sneeze, and I don't remember ever feeling cold.

I don't think that at that time I had ever felt unhappy either. In some moods the country seemed compounded of azure and gold. In the mornings – the very early mornings by the sea – the chill that rose from the water was comforted by the promise of warmth as the sun grew stronger, and all the world seemed balanced and perfect, light and clear with that blue-gold radiance, cool and warm, like silk: it happened in early summer before the hordes arrived. Honeysuckle and wild roses hung with the fuchsia and ivy over the stone walls, still in the windless air, and all the day lay ahead. After that, inevitably, the day came as something of an anticlimax, filled with people and events, and the perfect balance was lost.

One evening – it must have been a Sunday, since we were having cold meat and home-made chutney for supper – the man who kept the pig-farm beside the railway line, just north of the gasworks, called to show us an orphaned lamb which I, being very young and stupid, named Black Paws. It behaved in the thoughtless way usual with sheep, which made Primrose cross. Somebody told me lambs had hooves not paws. I had fallen in love with the thing when Alfie Ellis said he had to take it away again, and later I made the connection between the living lamb and the meat we had had with the chutney for supper. Perhaps my acute dislike of Sunday evenings dates from then. Alfie Ellis was married to the district nurse who was a great friend of my cousin's, which is entirely irrelevant, but I have just remembered and so I pass on the information.

MANY YEARS LATER another house on the same road was sold when the owner, a widow who had done some cleaning for my mother, had sung in the church choir and been a prominent helper in the local jumble sales, decided to move. The new owners – new brooms as new owners always are – opening a bricked-up doorway discovered the cause of her widowhood. There lay the bones of her husband whom she had killed and, presumably, had chosen to forget about. The usual inquiry followed, and his family were understandably mad with rage; she claimed it was done in self-defence and was given a suspended sentence, and the whole matter faded from public view. I said I had always felt that death stalked that stretch of road (except, when you come to think about it, death stalks everywhere), but what I found really strange was not that she had killed him and told nobody, nor even that she had lived with his hidden body for all that time, but that she had gone away leaving him to be discovered. It almost seemed as though he, and the Deed, mattered to her so little that she thought it of no importance. Perhaps that blighted stretch of road is distinguished, not by the presence of death, but by an absence of the awareness of its meaning; then again, perhaps not.

The road round Penmaenmawr has long been perceived as violent and inhospitable. When the Romans attempted it the then inhabitants threw boulders down on them. Dr Johnson, Daniel Defoe, Dean Swift and many others spoke of it with abhorrence as Awful, Hideous, Precipitous, Horrid; and clearly parts of it used to be dangerous, the mountainside bulging out over a narrow track before it swept down to yet more rocks and the ravenous waves, and bits of it constantly falling off, but I still think they exaggerated. There have been dreadful accidents along it, but there are dreadful

accidents everywhere, not least on wide motorways. Besides, the stretch that I see as deadly is the flat part between Dwygyfylchi and Penmaenan, not the parts they complained of. I have fond memories of returning home at night from Llandudno or Bangor in a warm and lighted bus, round and under the overhanging rocks which Dr Johnson hated with such a passion.

In 1806 one Mavor wrote of

> the abrupt and tremendous cliffs of Penmaenmawr, which are computed to rise 1550 feet in perpendicular height, above the level of the sea. On a ledge of this cliff, by an excellent but frightful road, though defended by a stone wall about five feet high, we wind round the mountain; while the vast impending rocks above our heads, the roaring of the waves at a great distance below, the howling of the wind and the beating of the rain, all united to fill the mind with solemnity and awe.

Quite recently two hitch-hikers were travelling this road when their driver stopped and stepped over the aforesaid wall to relieve himself. He never came back, poor man. As Mavor puts it: 'A stone thrown over the precipice into the sea with all our might, seemed to drop at the very foot of the rocks.' He goes on: 'No stranger ever passed this way without fear, not withstanding all the precautions that have been taken to render it secure: but as the great Irish road is now carried through Capel Cerrig, the pass of Penmaen Mawr will in future be visited by comparatively few.'

Wrong, Mavor. Mavor was, if a hater of mountains, a lover of roads:

> The present road was made in 1772 under the direction of a person of the name of Sylvester, and it is a monument of his talents and perseverance. It forms the most sublime terrace in the British Isles.

Wrong again, Mavor. It has dwindled into insignificance alongside the Expressway. After some further insults and grousing – 'this awful promontory', 'it would be horrible to travel over this space' – he goes on to Conwy to grumble some more:

'Within the fortifications Conwy has a confined and gloomy appearance.' And there we will leave him.

More recent tourists found the solid traffic jams inconvenient. But tourists are, in themselves, death to the countryside, and should be discouraged, if not by dropping boulders on them at least by keeping the ways fairly impassable. Holidaymakers used to be another matter. Holidaymakers would go on the train to where they wished to be. They would stay in hotels or boarding houses or little houses offering B & B. They would take the local bus to places of interest, or walk around on their feet, and paddle in the sea and suck ice-creams, and go home again on the train when the time was ripe. They did not go round and round in motorcars destroying the silent and the secret places, and hauling caravans and demanding that four-lane highways be instantly constructed for their convenience. They did not permanently alter the local way of life which, when they had gone, resumed its normal tenor.

Francis Kilvert felt the same way about tourists. As he remarked on visiting Llanthony in 1870:

> Of all noxious animals too, the most noxious is a tourist. And of all tourists the most vulgar, ill-bred, offensive and loathsome is the British tourist.

They didn't mince their words in those days.

WE WENT TO live in a cottage on the top road between the Iron Age axe factory of Graiglwyd and the granite quarry. I could see the sea from the bedroom window and the mountain rose behind us. We had plenty of books, there were a number of congenial children living nearby and if it hadn't been for the necessity of going to school I should have been entirely content.

The water came from a tap in the backyard below the garden and gave forth tadpoles in season. One summer the reservoir dried up and I had to get water in a bucket from a spring on *ffrith* (which means, more or less, the lower part of a mountain – pasture

land). It was very difficult, for the sun had made the turf as slippery as glass and you also had to climb over a fence with a strand of barbed wire on top of it, which was deleterious to the nether garments when you were hampered by a heavy, brimming pail. There were a lot of vipers around that summer too.

The lavatory was also in a shed in the backyard. It had a broad wooden seat and on this seat were all too frequently to be discovered slugs, basking in the dim chill of the dripping, moss-covered walls. Many of them were enormous; some spotted like the pard, some striped, all slimy, revolting and with a baleful air. We kept a piece of wood in there to push them down the pan, but I used often not to warn guests of the hazard they presented. There would be frightful screams and ladies would fly out, ashen-faced. The enlightened used always to take a torch and thoroughly scrutinise the premises before making any rash moves such as sitting down. We bathed in a tin bath in front of the range or in our friends' more well-appointed houses. The nain of one of my friends had the curious habit of running your bath for you, throwing in the better part of a packet of soap powder and a generous slurp of Dettol. It was doubtless very cleansing but it made you smell funny. You were never permitted to go home until your hair had dried and were always given tea and *bara brith* or bread and butter to fortify you against the elements after this dangerous immersion in warm water.

I still know people in the district who regard bathing as a risky business. Everyone did at one time, but I do all my best thinking in the bath. It used to be frustrating having a concerned nain or mam or auntie banging anxiously on the door after five minutes in case you should ruin your health by lying too long in the water. I have a theory that people kept their coal in the bath not because they were unaware of the true purpose of this receptacle, but because they were unwilling to dice with death by getting into it themselves. Nevertheless everyone was very clean. A lot of the village ladies would wash themselves from top to toe in sections before going down to Pantyrafon, the main shopping street, in the afternoon on a shopping expedition.

We had a small front garden with a little wooden gate and a slate path. There was a lilac tree on the left with banks of snow-in-summer growing underneath it. On the right was a fuchsia hedge and my mother tried to grow dahlias but the sheep used to jump down the wall from the mountain and eat them. I never used the gate in the evenings. There was a toehold in the wall and with one bound you were free and up on *ffrith*. With my whole body I can remember that toehold.

I WENT TO the National School on the coast road and, since Penmaenmawr slopes as it does, my first classroom was half underground. In the winter it was warmed by an open stove and we did our sums on wood-framed slates using slate pencils which, licked and held in a certain way, made the sort of noise that drives some people mad – like a long fingernail scratching a nylon stocking. Certain of my friends, having discovered the power of this noise, would slide the last part of the road to school down the slate-lined gutters with a granite chipping under foot.

I had enemies too. There was a boy called Robert who lived in Penmaenan (all our enemies lived in Penmaenan, which was out of bounds except for raiding parties) who had thick glasses and a chronic dribble, and used to chase me round the playground. He caught me and kissed me one day, and I was reprimanded by the headmaster, who said he would never have expected such a thing of me. I have never recovered from the injustice of this and I hope Robert has had a rotten life. Then there was a little English boy whose name I never knew, who didn't even attempt to fraternise with the natives but played trains all by himself, going *choo choo* and working his elbows like pistons. The badder boys jeered at him in the playground and he once made a response so dignified and so touching that I wept. I can't remember what it was, but the memory still brings tears to my eyes. I daresay today I should want to smack him.

As time went by our teacher, G.O. Jones, taught us, among other things, to write properly, with a pen. This involved penholders and nibs and wipers and ink monitors whose duty it was to refill the inkwells on each desk, which must have been quite tricky since most of us used them as receptacles for the cod-liver oil capsules and iron pills which a caring authority deemed necessary for our health. G.O. had been gassed in the First World War and as a result he spat a bit as he spoke, and our exercise books came up in moisture bubbles when he stood beside us. He, too, had trouble with Robert whose mother used to burst in roaring when her boy had been quite correctly caned. G.O. said she was a *blackguard* and I admired this sophisticated choice of words, although I wouldn't have cared to cross her myself. There were several women like this around, gypsy-like and intimidating, and quite unlike the majority who wore black straw hats and gloves to Chapel and high-necked, black garments and never swore.

The most remarkable of the foul-mouthed ladies lived near us on the top road in a cottage which stood – or rather was falling down – on its own. She was called Bonny Mary and she had a brother called John Tom who was mad. He spoke to no one but himself and would stride, stick in hand, along the top road jumping, at intervals, into the air, glaring and gesturing and concerned only with some private irritating matter. Many people used to take their constitutionals along the top road: the nuns from the local convent and Father Hugh from the Franciscan friary. Bonny Mary had a son and daughter too and they all slept, as far as we could tell, on heaps of sacks and old newspapers. There was very little furniture to be seen through the open door. I don't think her children went to school. I never saw them there. She was considered to be a witch.

There were many witches in Wales. The nastiest was the Gwrach y Rhibyn who was about ten feet tall and whose breath killed you. Then there were two sisters who kept an inn with a bad reputation near Llandudno. They used to turn themselves into cats and steal the guests' gold and watches, which I would have thought would be easier to accomplish if you retained your human form, your fingers and pockets – but it wouldn't make such a good story. They came to the usual end. One intrepid traveller stayed awake, whacked the prowling cat on the leg with a stick and, lo and behold, next morning one of the ladies pronounced herself incommoded and unable to come down to breakfast. When she did appear she had a shocking limp.

Two other sisters who lived in the foothills of Snowdonia were themselves bothered by a cat-witch. They had had a very plain serving maid who fell in love with the *fiancé* of one of them. Perhaps this made her dreamy, for she was sacked for incompetence and thrown out to live in a cave and sustain herself as best she could on stolen turnips from the fields. Shortly afterwards the sisters exhibited fearful scratches on their faces and it was decided that the aggrieved maid had transformed herself into a cat and devoted herself to ruining their beauty. I myself think it more likely that both sisters were in love with the *fiancé* and the scratches were the result of sibling rivalry and strife. Clearly, however, it would have been more dignified and acceptable to the family if they could put the blame on the cat. Cats, being such beautiful creatures, sufficient unto themselves, have always aroused envy in human beings. Too often people resort to kicking the cat.

School became more onerous as the scholarship approached. My first teacher, Miss Roberts, a dear feathery old person, had let me draw fairies when I should have been doing sums and I never did get the hang of the things, so I was made to go for private lessons to Mr Pugh, an ex-schoolteacher who lived with his wife in a cold, clean house with a ticking clock. These lessons were hell – as much, I imagine, for the unfortunate Pugh as they were for me – since I was incapable even of short division and simply couldn't see the point. He asked, one day, as I seemed not to be concentrating, if I was frightened of him and I explained that it was just that I'd rather be playing with the Joneses on the clinker pile outside the laundry. Clinkers were what was left of the coke which fed the boilers, and it has only just occurred to me to wonder why they were dumped on the roadside and not taken away. I don't remember the pile ever getting any smaller.

This laundry also stood on the top road and the washing was hung to dry in the field behind. We thought it the height of wit to take in live shrews (which we took off the cats) to frighten the laundry girls who all, so the local wisdom went, had perfect complexions from working in a steamy atmosphere. Jack Laundry drove the van and his wife, Jenny Laundry, made perfect chutney. Chutney was an important aspect of life in Penmaenmawr.

The Joneses – there were six of them, but the little ones didn't count much in those days – had evolved a complex and fast-moving game with a ball and the clinker heap. People were stationed at various points and heights on the clinkers, the ball went round and you took it from there. It seems perverse to have been playing on the detritus from the laundry boilers with the Snowdon range beginning behind us, but it was nearer home and our mothers could call us in for tea without having to trudge up Moelfre. The Jones children had evolved a noise – a war whoop – by which we could recognise and discover each other up on the hills. It was quite difficult to do, starting low in the throat and rising, but was effective once mastered.

I now feel nostalgic for that school by the sea. We were taught calmly and authoritatively what our teachers deemed it necessary for us to know, and often in the afternoons G.O. would tell us stories – not read out from books, but the living legends of the locality. The oral tradition was still strong then, and I can think of no better start in life for a person who is going to end up as a writer. I hated sums, and the warm milk we had to drink at playtime (we used to try and shake the little bottle until the milk turned into butter – something the Celts have been doing since the dawn of history, not in bottles, naturally, but in skins and churns and anything which could be agitated), and Robert, who took to throwing stones at me (I still bear the scars), and being caned, which didn't happen often but was painful when it did (you were advised by your peers

to spit in the hand which was going to take the punishment and lay two hairs from your head crosswise over the spit, but it didn't work), but I liked the darkening winter afternoons with the iron stove glowing and the endless stories. I think I was fortunate.

ON SUNDAYS WE weren't allowed to play. Everyone went to Church or Chapel and an air of melancholy lay over the land. In the past the villagers had had an

awful warning which possibly made them even more careful than the rest of Wales. There were three women (the Welsh have a habit of thinking in triads) whose task it was to winnow the wheat. I don't know where they got it from. Not a lot of wheat was grown in Penmaenmawr by the time I arrived. Perhaps it came from Anglesey, the bread-basket of Wales, or perhaps this was before the inundation and it grew on the plains where the sea now lies. However it grew, such was these three women's enthusiasm that they wanted to winnow it even on Sundays against the strong advice of their more god-fearing neighbours. Perhaps they found Sundays as tedious as I did.

Whatever happened, there they were, devoured by this overwhelming urge to winnow wheat, and there was no breeze. It was a still, hot day such as we don't often see in Wales, but instead of making the most of it and going for a paddle, or lying down in the long grass, they had the daft idea of carrying it to the top of Moelfre, where, they reasoned, there was bound to be a wind. So they each carried a heavy sack of wheat up the hill, one wearing a white apron, one a red and one a blue. They had just discovered the breeze to be perfect and had set about their task when an irate deity turned them to stone. The three stone women have now sunk into the ground.

I never felt that this was a Christian or even an Old Testament deity (who hadn't taken such swift or irrational offence since Lot's wife) but another, even more irascible force. Strange gods have been worshipped on those hills, whose laws have been long forgotten. It was widely taken for granted that once upon a time people with red hair were sacrificed up there by, so the rumour went, the Druids: but the ring of standing stones known as the Druid's Circle is older than that cult and its purpose unknown. Excavations have uncovered burial chambers round about (one containing the bones of a small person) and while all this was perfectly fine on a bright summer's day – merely a matter of history, superstition and the past – a bank of clouds, a sudden mist or the onset of dusk could quite radically alter one's point of view.

Even *ffrith*, the mountain slope behind our cottages, which we knew as well as the palms of our hands, could turn very strange with the shades of night, and sometimes I would arrive home out of breath. You could always remark that your mother would be mad if you were late, since while none of us would readily admit to being afraid of the mountain-walker it was perfectly respectable to obey your mam – as long as you didn't go to ridiculous lengths. I don't know where the concept of the mountain-walker arose – I've never found him in a book – but for many years, and possibly even now, it was the thought of him that got me down off the mountain in good time for supper. What he did, as his name would imply, was walk the mountains all the time, to and fro, every now and then pausing to despatch an unwary shepherd or benighted traveller. He was the biggest of all the giants, which is odd as the stories would have us believe that the giants were disposed of centuries ago together with the *gwiberod*, the *afanc* and the

witches. (The Tylwyth Teg and the Cŵn Annwn lingered longer and, for all I know, may still be around. The knockers certainly are, for I've heard them.) But to get back to the giant. It was unlikely that you'd be sufficiently unlucky to meet him for he had all the mountains of Wales to cover, but the possibility was always there and every now and then people did disappear without trace. The mountain slopes, so sweet with heather and bilberry and gorse, give way to bleak moorland, bog and precipice, and the mists that descend without warning.

WHEN I WAS very young, before I learned about fear, I used to climb the mountains, clad in sensible shorts, with my father and his friends. They carried maps and sandwiches and tin things for making tea in and it was all nicely organised. I remember whining as we plodded up the steep, stony, fly-haunted lane that led to the Green Gorge: 'When will we get to the *grass?*' But once we were there I was as good as gold. I know because I've been told so. I could walk for miles, squelching over the bog cotton and the sphagnum moss, climbing over stiles and dry-stone walls. There were wild goats and mountain ponies, and sometimes, in the spring, we would go to the Old Church of Llangelynyn where the tiny wild daffodils grew.

We walked on the lower slopes of Snowdon and sometimes we camped with Primrose's husband, the scoutmaster and his scouts, but I can't remember much about it – only tea with condensed milk, little fires and the sound of streams. We never tackled any rocks and nobody mentioned the mountain-walker. They sang songs – 'Sospan Fach' and 'The Quartermaster's Stores' – and when we came home I always had grass in my hair.

We used to go to tea at the farm with Primrose's in-laws in Roewen. We had warm, boiled mutton and bread and butter and tea, which I found strange, being more accustomed to marmite sandwiches, but it was very acceptable at the time. They always used to give me an illustrated book of Bible stories to read and then a lady – I think it was probably somebody's aunt, but I've never been any good at figuring out precise relationships – would question me about them. Curiously enough I rather enjoyed

this. The farmhouses had high-backed wooden settles, dressers and ranges with black cauldrons, but since then I have met too many people who have told me their mam got fed up with the old-fashioned things and threw them out in favour of more comfortable furniture, convenience and ease.

The Welsh approach to food was simple. Mostly you boiled it. In the last century, bread and butter, and various forms of gruel, *siot*, *sucan*, flummery and porridge were the staples, at least among the poor hill-farmers. Occasionally they had cheese and

salted meat, boiled perhaps with cabbage or leeks; but they couldn't afford to eat their own fresh meat because that had to be sold. I know this because I read it in a book. Things had improved by the time I came on the scene although the underlying approach remained the same, and I've never yet met a Celt who could scramble an egg. They always end up with a lump of rubbery curd and a lot of warm water. On the other hand nobody can bake like the Celts, and they are skilled in the use of the griddling iron. Welsh cakes and *crempogau* are wonderful, and the different sorts of bread and scones are unmatched by the average Saxon. I have an idea that the swift little Celts only had time to boil or griddle something in an iron pot over an open fire before running away from a marauding party or forming a marauding party of their own, whereas the sanguine Saxon sat around making earthenware pots and simmering casseroles in them. There is some truth in this, but I may as well say now that my grasp of history is tenuous and that those in search of factual accuracy would be well advised to look elsewhere.

The *boneddigion*, of course, fared better, as the upper classes always do. Leaping ahead to the eighteenth century, the following is the bill of fare at the 'entertainment' given by Sir Watkin Williams Wynn at Wynnstay to celebrate the coming of age of his son in April 1770, as described in *Archaeologia Cambrensis*:

> 30 bullocks; one roasted whole; 50 hogs, 50 calves, 80 sheep, 18 lambs, 70 pies, 51 guinea fowls, 37 turkeys, 12 turkey-poult, 84 capons, 24 pie-fowls, 300 chickens, 360 fowls, 96 ducklings, 48 rabbits, 15 snipes, 1 leveret, 5 bucks, 242 pounds of salmon, 50 brace of tench, 40 brace of carp, 36 pike, 60 dozen of trout, 108 flounders, 109 lobster, 96 crabs, 10 quarts of shrimps, 200 crawfish, 60 barrels of pickled oysters, 1 hogs-head of rock-oysters, 20 quarts of oysters for sauce, 166 hams, 100 tongues, 125 plum-puddings, 34 rice-puddings, 7 venison pies, 60 raised pies, 80 tarts, 30 pieces of cut pastry, 24 pound cakes, 60 Savoy cakes, 30 sweetmeat-cakes, 12 backs of bacon, 144 ice-creams, 18,000 eggs, 150 gallons of milk, 60 quarts of cream, 30 bushels of potatoes, 6,000 asparagus, 200 French beans, 3 dishes of green peas, 12 cucumbers, 70 hogs-heads of ale, 120 dozen of wine, brandy, rum . . . It is thought that there were at least 15,000 people at dinner.

DURING THE WAR everybody's eating habits changed. Living in the country we were minimally better off than some. Our back garden supported a gooseberry bush and a wilderness of rhubarb and mint, and the neighbours gave us lettuces and cabbages. I have never understood why people grow so many cabbages. A row of twenty burgeoning simultaneously must surely tax the capabilities of even the most vitamin-conscious family, and everyone grew them in rows of at least twenty. In season we picked bilberries, wild raspberries, blackberries, damsons, crab apples and nuts, and I once found a hen's egg in a hedgerow but my mother made me give it back to the farmer, Dick Graiglwyd, which I thought over-scrupulous of her. Eggs in the war were scarcer than hen's teeth. For some reason she didn't mind occasionally buying black-market farm butter, perhaps because this was seen merely as chiselling the authorities and was not in the same class as theft from the farmer, being paid for. I didn't like it. It was greasy and salty and when you stuck a knife in it water squirted out.

There were sometimes rumours that somebody had killed one of his pigs and was hiding the carcase in the baby's cradle, or smoking it, concealed amongst the washing on the rack over the range. You were not permitted to kill a pig without permission, supervision and the filling in of forms which, not unnaturally, seized the heart of the pig-owner with resentment. I have heard of people reminiscing wistfully about the days when pigs were publicly stuck in Pantyrafon. You could, they said, hear them squealing for miles. I was glad those days had passed. In one of the fields below our cottage there was a stone slaughterhouse. Standing on tiptoe you could see great hooks hanging from the ceiling, and often dogs would be locked in there, howling. It was an unfriendly place, implicit with pain and fear and the memory of blood. Once there was a sheep's head in the brambles by the back road. It stayed there for days, glaring mournfully through the prickles. And once I thought I found a human ear on some waste ground in the dread Penmaenan, but looking back I think I must have been mistaken.

On the whole we were protected from the more brutal aspects of life on the farm. Lambing, sheep dipping and shearing, haymaking and the heaving up of turnips held no terrors for the delicately reared; and watching the man boiling the pig mash out of doors on an autumn evening was the sort of pleasure that you might remember on your

deathbed. A fine cold, clear autumn evening is the sort of thing you might remember on your deathbed anyway, and combined with this was the illicit delight of being up past your bedtime, with night coming down over the mountains and yet being safe with the bonfire crackling and lighting up the low branches of the hazel trees and the men stirring the swill and talking to each other. Then a run across the field back to the cottage fireside, tingling, as they say, with well-being. I never feel like that any more.

OUT IN THE bay, underneath the sea, lie the remains of Llys Helig, once a castle and a town surrounded by meadows and orchards and fields of grain. An idyllic spot, except that, as so often happens, its ruler was a truly nasty piece of work, who spread fear and corruption throughout the land. He had respect neither for God nor man and never drew a sober breath. He gave the sort of parties that last all week, inciting his guests to behave worse and worse until they lay around in heaps, exhausted, comatose and blind with liquor. He was warned several times by the more responsible members of the community that this behaviour could lead to no good. The harpist in particular was loud in his protests and denunciations (for some reason harpists always were), but the ruler took no notice, apart from killing a few people who he considered had gone too far and were too impudent and irritating to live. His subjects cowered in their huts, bowed down with apprehension, fearing both the wrath of their overlord and the dreadful consequences that his Cities-of-the-Plain lifestyle would bring upon them all.

Unearthly voices were heard in the night, crying vengeance, and no one slept easy in his bed, nor was able, in the morning, to take untroubled delight in the loveliness of the fertile fields and groves. One evening during the course of an orgy, spectacular even by his standards, the sky grew prematurely dark.

'Looks like rain,' said Helig, staring with unfocused eyes at the deepening shadows. 'Have another drink.'

His five wolfhounds, three dogs and two bitches, who had been lying sucking the marrow out of some venison bones, got up from the floor, all strewn as it was with decaying rushes and the remains of old feasts, and began to pace uneasily up and down, sniffing the wind and whimpering.

'Lie down, you dogs,' roared their master. 'Heel.'

But they had leapt up the steps of the great chamber and were streaking towards the hills, the hair on the back of their necks sticking up straight. The ruler rallied a moment from his stupor to promise himself he would flay them alive when they came back, and called for another barrel of mead.

'Storm at sea,' he muttered, as the skies grew darker and the shadows crept closer.

The old manservant doddered, rush light in hand, down through the blackness to where the drink was kept. He was up again in no time, shaking with shock, and his feet wet.

'Sire, Sire,' he gasped, 'the fishes are swimming in the cellars.'

'Don't be such a bloody fool,' said Helig, 'or I'll have your ears cut off.'

Trembling, the old man contrived to drag a barrel into the banqueting hall. Already the mead tasted of salt, but Helig was too far gone to notice.

'Aargh,' said the old man after a while, 'Sire, the fishes are swimming about your feet.'

'If you don't shut up,' roared Helig, 'I'll have your eyes put out.'

He clambered on to a low dais where the harpist had been wont to sit, strumming his warnings and singing his lays. He quaffed his mead and gazed, half-seeing, at his unconscious guests lying all around. They did look a bit damp and the fire had gone out.

'Superstitious nonsense,' grumbled Helig to himself, trying to draw his feet up out of the sea.

'Sire, Sire,' screamed the old manservant, who had prudently left the castle, uttering his third warning, 'the fishes are swimming through the windows.'

'If you say that once more,' whispered Helig, 'I'll cut off your – glug, glug, glug . . .'

The sober and industrious peasants had gathered up whatever they could carry and had fled, led by the harpist and the old manservant, away from the waves which had first crept and then tumbled all over their lands, and crouched, wringing their hands and blind with weeping, at a place called Trwyn y Wylfa – The Point of Wailing – high on the hill.

I have had tea at the farmhouse there too. Sometimes at low tide you can see the gaunt remains of Helig's castle – or perhaps it's only a natural rock formation. Who knows? The past is inaccessible to us and all we have is the stories the old men tell. Or perhaps it is all true and the accursed Helig is responsible still for the sense of death that hangs over that stretch of road. If his unquiet spirit still walks beneath the waves out there I wonder what it will make of the four-lane highway – or, as it is called, the Expressway. I suppose one could take the view that it will serve him right.

Curiously enough Helig's five sons, Gwynan, Celynin, Peris, Frothen and Rhychwyn, were very good men. I don't know where they were when the sea came in, but they all survived and added lustre to the sixth-century church. (At that time North Wales 'glittered with churches as the firmament with stars'.) Nor do I know why such a bad man should have generated a brood of children who were well-behaved to the point that when they died they were all 'canonised for sainctes'. Such an eventuality gives one furiously to think about our modern theories on the upbringing of the young. Neither by virtue of nature or nurture would one have supposed that Helig's offspring could turn out as anything but a bunch of total delinquents, let alone 'sainctes'. I wonder what a psychiatrist would make of it. I find it rather reassuring. The drunkard, Seithenyn, keeper of the dyke, also fathered a saint, St Tudno. I know nothing of the mothers of all those holy men but can only suppose that their influence outweighed that of their husbands.

ONE OF THE benefits of this road is said to be that it will save the town of Conwy from falling over, shaken to shards by the volume of traffic in its narrow streets. Already the street fairs have had to go in the interests of the motor-car, and the place isn't the same. Not even the same as it was ten years ago. The street markets were for the local people and have gone in order to make life easier for the tourist. Everywhere there are shops selling things for tourists, instructions to guide tourists to places of interest, cafés cooking things for tourists to eat and places for tourists to park their cars. While one does not wish to become unhinged on the subject, it must be said that the 'noxious animal', the tourist, and the locust have much in common, destroying what they feed upon and rendering whole districts barren and pointless. I have recently heard it suggested that the benefits which tourists seem to bestow are undone by the cost of catering for their whims and repairing the depredations they cause. It is, however, dishonest to hanker after the days of Llewelyn without reminding oneself that then there was no running hot water, and even if there were no tourists as such there were warring princes fighting for territory everywhere and soaking the land with blood.

In the sixteenth century a dreadful thing happened in Plas Mawr, the mansion in the High Street. The master, Sir Robert Wynne, had been away smiting the foe, for the bloodshed went on and on, and when he was expected home his wife, who was pregnant with her second child, went upstairs with her little boy to watch for him from a window (there are 365 in Plas Mawr).

He didn't turn up. So, as night drew on, she began to make her way down, when she missed her footing and plunged to the foot of the stairs, holding her little boy by the hand and thus dragging him with her.

The servants in a great panic sent for the family doctor, but unfortunately he was out and a young locum, Doctor Dic, arrived in his stead. He had just left medical school and lacked the confidence of long experience. He was wholly daunted by the situation and dithered around, wrung his hands and pled a previous engagement, but the servants, who also sound rather useless (nobody even seems to have had the wit to boil a lot of water – the usual inevitable prelude to childbearing), pushed him into the room, told him to do what he could and scuttled downstairs, where they sat, rocking back and forth with their aprons over their heads and calling on the Lord to preserve them. The butler, showing a bit of sense, sent the ostler to scour the neighbourhood for the old family doctor, and they all waited.

Time passed: there was an ominous silence in the *accouchement* chamber, when suddenly there came a great knock on the door. With glad relief a maidservant flung it open, but it wasn't the doctor. It was Sir Robert, who had forgotten his key. Piecing together what had happened from the incoherent ramblings of his menials he rushed to his wife only to find her lying dead with her premature babe, and his little son dead too. When the servants had gathered enough courage to go and look they found that Sir Robert had committed suicide with his dagger. Of Doctor Dic there was no sign. The theory is that he had climbed up the chimney, leaving not so much as his stethoscope, and is still up there somewhere, smoked as a bloater. I have had terrible trouble with crows floating down the chimney, but the idea of a doctor up it is a novel one.

After many years the ostler came back.

'What kept you?' enquired the butler.

The ostler explained that as he was running down a narrow street towards the quay he had been set upon by a press-gang and had been around the world a few times since then. No, all was not roses in the past.

I, too, once fell downstairs when I was pregnant with my sixth child, carrying the then two-year-old on one arm. He and I were all right, but later the child was born prematurely and died. Pregnant women should be much, much more careful than Lady Wynne, or I. Mark my words. Medical science has made great strides, but we can't expect others to take the responsibility for our carelessness.

Poor Doctor Dic. It is said that Plas Mawr is haunted, and indeed there used to be a photograph of the ghost hanging there. Perhaps there still is. It was a modern, anglicised ghost in a sheet with holes for it to see through.

Welsh ghosts are rather different. On the road to Llandudno there is a hairy one who lives up a tree and leaps on to the backs of unwary passers-by, attempting to choke them and clinging for miles like the Old Man of the Sea. He is probably a version of the Ceffyl Dŵr – a phantom horse who can take many shapes, including that of a hairy, clinging frog, or indeed, probably, anything that occurred to him.

CONWY WAS ALWAYS a fishing village and mussel-gathering was one of its industries. Sometimes pearls dropped out of these mussels, which was lucky (except that it is said that these pearls attracted the Roman invader), but the local fishermen once contrived to get themselves and their descendants cursed in perpetuity, which was not. A mermaid got washed up on the rocks and called to them to refloat her. They refused and stood slapping their thighs with their hands all salt-hardened and covered in fish scales, laughing and pointing the finger, for they were ambivalent about the sea and the creatures thereof, since while it gave them their living it had taken from them fathers, brothers, friends, and they had, themselves, gone in fear of their lives in their little boats as the sea turned savage. The mermaid, as she expired, promised them floods and gales, wrecks and disasters.

Before Thomas Telford bridged the Conwy, people had either to cross at low tide – a dangerous enterprise – or wait for the ferry. Ferrymen seem to have been a worryingly unreliable group of men, frequently drunk on duty and deaf to frantic hails from the other side. Our eighteenth-century travellers had trouble with them at both Conwy and Beaumaris, roaring for the boat as the tide rose. Their inebriate habits are perhaps understandable. Waiting around in the wind and the rain for customers must have been tedious and uncomfortable, so they took refuge in the inn. Innkeepers are notoriously averse to patrons who linger over one little drink, taking up space by the fire, and the ferrymen would have had nothing to do but get steadily paralytic.

The castle is standing up well considering the vicissitudes of time, battles and vandalism. We were told in school that the secret of the mortar which holds all Welsh castles together has been forgotten. It was, said G.O., a particularly splendid and durable mortar with a secret ingredient – possibly human blood, possibly strong ale – but nobody knows any more. He spoke wistfully of this mortar as though it symbolised a lost and glorious past. Matthew Arnold wrote:

> Over the mouth of the Conway and its sands is the eternal softness and mild light of the West; the low line of the mystic Anglesey and the precipitous Penmaenmawr, and the great group of Carnedd Llywelyn and Carnedd Dafydd and their brethren fading away, hill behind hill, in an aerial haze, make the horizon; between the foot of Penmaenmawr and the bending coast of Anglesey, the sea, a silver stream, disappears one knows not whither. On this side, Wales: Wales, where the past still lives, where every place has its tradition, every name its poetry, and where the people – the genuine people – still knows this past, this tradition, this poetry, and lives with it, and clings to it; while, alas! the prosperous Saxon on the other side, the invader from Liverpool and Birkenhead, has long forgotten his. And the promontory where Llandudno stands is the very centre of this tradition; it is Creuddyn, the *bloody* city, where every stone has its story; there opposite its decaying rival, Conway Castle, is Deganwy, not decaying, but long since utterly decayed, some crumbling foundations on a crag top, and nothing more; Deganwy, where Maelgwn, the British prince, shut up Elphin, and where Taliesin came to free him.

Taliesin wouldn't half be surprised if he visited Deganwy now. Last time we were round there we had fish and chips from a genuine Chinese take-away.

I have a nineteenth-century book entitled *Welsh Pictures* which recommends the view from the base of Foel Lûs mountain. I quote again:

> From an eminence a little beyond the junction of the roads, a splendid view of the coast and the sea is obtained. On our right we see Llandudno and the Great

Orme . . . to our left we see the semicircular sweep of the splendid beach of which Penmaenmawr can justly boast [not any more it can't] and towering above its limit stands the great Penmaen itself, forming in its bold outline and with its beetling rocks the finest headland in Wales.

Not any more it doesn't. They've been blasting at it for ever, but there used to be a lump on top which popular wisdom held was sacrosanct: a monument, a landmark.

That's gone. One could almost think of it as Dr Johnson's revenge since he was so frightened edging his way round the overhang and disliked it so much.

How do these things happen? Who was first permitted to start removing this major aspect of the landscape? What would happen if an entrepreneur proposed to reduce, say, the Matterhorn by thousands of feet in order to use its substance to make roads? Admittedly quarrying has been going on in Penmaenmawr for some 5000-odd years, but while it may be necessary, and indeed seems quite reasonable to burrow away at the flanks of a famous mountain, it seems extraordinary to swipe off its summit as you would a boiled egg. There was once an ancient fort up there – Braich y Ddinas – where the Ordovicians hung out and which the Romans conquered. That's gone too. Sir John Wynne described the fortress as having threefold walls, nine feet thick, a hundred circular towers and room for 20,000 men.

But then people avid for roads have destroyed more than the 'great city' on Penmaenmawr. By the Highway Act of William IV in 1835 the road surveyor was given *carte blanche* to whip away any old stone he took a fancy to. There were hundreds of cromlechs on Anglesey which were dynamited out of the earth and hauled off to make roads. The surveyor could go almost anywhere in his quest for stone, and often farmers and landowners would be only too delighted to be spared the necessity of ploughing round some boring old prehistoric stone monument and happy to see it go.

I quote again from *Welsh Pictures*:

> Penmaenmawr is a watering-place, well known to most visitors to Llandudno, and a favourite resort with people who find the bustle and the noise of the latter place an annoyance. Its sheltered situation . . . walled in as it is by a circle of mountains and blessed with abundance of foliage, makes Penmaenmawr a very desirable spot for invalids and people in search of quiet rest.

The poor place now is a curious cross between a ghost town and a new town with half the shops in Pantyrafon closed down, and a spread of what I believe is known as 'housing development'. Those in search of rest would be well advised to stay at home.

When I was a child I was untroubled by the existence of the adjacent quarry. Every day a whistle would sound, followed by a bang as they blew up a bit more of it. Sometimes a gloom would hang over the village because a quarryman had been killed or injured; and blackberries picked in its vicinity had to be well washed under the tap in the back yard because they were covered with white quarry dust, but it was a fact of life and taken for granted.

Sometimes a man reputed to own it would ride with a woman, not his wife, along the top road on a huge, glossy horse and the children sitting on *ffrith* would jump up and down and jeer. His granddaughter married one of my cousins, and the last I heard she was sitting by his deathbed. Oh dear.

In the evenings, if the fancy took us, we would go and play in the more thrilling parts of the quarry. The Jones boys tied a long rope to a tree branch, and you sat on a knot at the bottom and swung out over a pit. I can still smell that rope and feel its fraying threads. You could sleigh on the seat of your pants down heaps of chippings, and the naughtier boys would try and ride the wagons but they were usually too well-secured. In the daytime the wagons went constantly up and down to the quarry boats moored at the jetty. That's gone, and so have the boats.

THE SCHIZOPHRENIC NATURE of existence in Penmaenmawr was enhanced on Sundays when noisy games were frowned upon. Nearly everybody went to some place of worship – some Chapel-goers went three times, hatted and gloved. I had to put aside the shorts and shirt which were my favoured mode of apparel and put on a frock – a symbol of freedom-loss. The air rang with hymn-singing and was redolent of boiled cabbage; I had never completed my homework and, of course, nobody was allowed out to play. It was a penitential day. Even now, even if I'm miles from the nearest habitation I know when it's Sunday in Wales: by the atmosphere. My father, for reasons known only to himself, had elected to join an organisation called the Church of Humanity, whose chief tenet was Positivism. It was a peculiarly unappealing doctrine. My mother went to St Seiriol's, the Church in Wales. I had a Sunday best friend, Mair, as opposed to the more turbulent weekday ones, and for a while I went with her and her nain to the English Congregational church, where on several occasions I was invited to read the lesson in Welsh. Looking back I find this mysterious, but there it was. Later I went to Chapel Sunday School, where we were given coloured pamphlets detailing the events in the Bible, but in those days I was a pagan, and it meant little to me except as stories.

In the afternoons Mair and I would walk to Dwygyfylchi and the Fairy Glen where her aunts lived in an old cottage by the waterfall. I quote yet again from *Welsh Pictures* (I am sorry about all this quotation, but the irony of it has me by the throat):

> At the head of the valley we have a Fairy Glen on a smaller scale than the famous spot bearing that designation at Bettws y Coed. There is only a small rivulet here, but the scenery presents many exquisite combinations of rock and wood and stream.

It was its very smallness that made it so magical. There was a rickety wooden bridge across the stream, birches, and larches hung with pink tassels; there were banks of moss, and bluebells and wood anemone, birds and rabbits.

Sometimes we walked there over the mountain – round the Jubilee Path and then through the bracken and bilberry bushes along a narrow path of turf, and down through the glen to the cottage of the aunts – and sometimes we walked along Conwy Old Road which was quicker but not so interesting. Sometimes, usually at Easter or Whitsuntide, adults would come with us, which entirely ruined the whole point of the exercise. They meant well but their presence was lowering to the spirits and I could never think of anything to say to them. Looking back I find it remarkable to realise how small a part adults played in our lives. Our fathers were mostly away at the war and our mothers, aunts and nains were simply part of the background.

We saw very little of the men who were not away at the war – the farmers and shepherds and quarrymen. They were always out or sitting silently over the fire while the women talked. I expect they were tired, but I always had the impression when I was a child that women actually ran everything: budgeting the money and making sure that people washed, had clean clothes for Sunday, and enough to eat. I had to tolerate the occasional 'treat', being taken to Rhyl or Liverpool or on the steamer to the Isle of Man, but I was always impatient to get the excursion over and done with so that I could be back before nightfall and up on *ffrith* with the other children, not tramping gloomily round some pleasure palace or fun-fair.

The Joneses, lucky things, were seldom taken anywhere because there were too many of them. When it was raining hard we played cards in their parlour, but we spent as little time as possible indoors. Even birthday parties were conducted on the hills and in the fields after the jelly and cake had been consumed. On my eighth birthday I sat in a cowpat wearing my best frock of pale green crêpe with pink roses on it. I hate birthdays and parties and having to make conversation and show appreciation on social occasions. Falling down in a cowpat somehow neatly symbolises one's semi-conscious feelings about the whole business. A year or so ago, wearing my present best frock of black velvet, I sat in some spilled champagne during a charity auction. Times change – but not all that much – and the sensation of a damp seat to the garments remains uniquely disagreeable.

*F*FRITH WAS A place of unrestricted freedom where you could run, leap, shout, slide, hide, jump on the unsuspecting enemy, or just go to sleep in the heather. Perhaps we picked up some lingering race memory from the 20,000 warriors who were round the same site all those years ago, rolling boulders and hacking intruders to ribbons with flints.

The Fairy Glen had a much calmer ambience. Mair and I played domestic games there with dolls, which the Joneses would have considered eccentric, if not sissy. I find it impossible to describe the balance between what we accepted as the perfect safety of the hills and sea and valleys, and the dangers that also undoubtedly lay just beyond the bounds of our own discretion. On the whole we knew how far we could go, and there was little to fear but the mountain-walker.

The fairies of the glen were, I think, creatures of an English imagination, little things with gossamer wings and acorn cups for hats. Welsh fairies – the Tylwyth Teg – more resembled the human race: miniature people with miniature horses and dogs. They were richly dressed in red and green and were ruled over by Gwyn ap Nudd. On the whole they were well disposed towards humans and would perform household tasks on receipt of a bowl of milk and some bread. I believe they lived in more remote places than the glen, up on the hills and even under them.

While this place hasn't actually gone it is no longer accessible. We went there a few months ago and trotted trustfully up the path from Dwygyfylchi, eagerly anticipating the first sight of the waterfall, but there was a gate across the path, locked. We turned round and went down again to ask in the pubs what was going on, but nobody seemed to know. All they knew was that somebody had bought the cottage and the land, and locked the gate. The aunts used to serve teas to visitors – bread and butter and scones and Welsh cakes – and we used to help by washing the plates in the stream. They had a pet sheep called Megan, and the cottage smelled of wood-smoke and water, of baking and sheep's wool and tea and heather. I don't suppose it does any more.

Two little children once lived on the tops not far from the head of the glen. They played in the heather, but one day they wandered too far and they died before they were found. They had left a little trail of the Christmas cards they'd been playing with, but it ran out too soon. It seemed like one of the terrible things that had happened in the past and been transmuted into fairy tale and thus rendered unreal, but our mothers had seen their mother and it was true. It never occurred to us to fear human beings despite the past and the horrors of history.

There was a police station on the Bangor Road but the only person I remember being arrested was the grandfather of one of my friends. He was drunk: not even disorderly – just sitting by the phone box outside the council gardens, gazing into space. My friend rather revelled in the reflected glory, 'Taid's in prison', but he was only kept in a police cell till he sobered up, and the rest of the family were far from pleased about it.

Then at some point the army did set up a shooting range not too far from Graiglwyd which rather curtailed our activities. All children were forbidden by parents and military alike to go anywhere within the bounds of this range, but a lot of them disobeyed. You could tell who they were because they had frequently blown off their eyebrows, playing with thunder flashes. They got yelled at by the teachers too when they appeared in school, balded and blackened, and told time and again that they could have been blinded.

Once a child fell asleep in a beach shelter and when his friends couldn't find him they went and told his mam he must have drowned. Children are so thoughtless.

AS I GREW older and could make my own decisions I stayed away from the beach in the summertime since it was thronged with people playing ball games, wriggling in and out of their clothes because they had just leapt or were about to leap in the ocean, making sand pies, paddling, eating the usual sandy sandwiches and looking, in our view, singularly fatuous. These were the 'Visitors', and the prime concern of all of us was never ever, under any circumstances, to be mistaken for one of them. I still feel like this. I hate being defined as a holidaymaker and I feel idiotic in foreign countries. The natives are usually patient and courteous and happy to take your money, but you know they'd be even happier if the necessity had not arisen, and will be glad to see the last of you.

Occasionally still I was instructed to join my mother and her friends on the leeward side of the slipway when I came out of school. We'd sit on towels on the inhospitable pebbles and eat picnic-type things while the wind came looking for us. It all felt oddly exposed and simultaneously constraining. You could not, for example, play cops-and-robbers or give vent to the war-whoop on the beach without upsetting a lot of people. All you could do was bathe and get dry, paddle or mess about with those boring, doomed sand-castles. Sometimes there were moments of slight excitement as unwary castle-makers realised that the tide had crept up on them and they'd have to swim back, but the beach *was* very safe and they usually made it.

I had at that time a mongrel called Rex, who afforded us a certain amount of quiet amusement. There were always some people sitting on the edge of the promenade, dangling their feet above the pebbles, and Rex, taking the course at a sort of brisk walk, would go along in a straight line, choosing his targets, lifting his leg and peeing down their spines. He could accomplish this without stopping and so smoothly that no one knew what was happening until it was too late.

I had a low-slung pony too, who regarded lorries, tractors and the Irish Mail with perfect insouciance but was rendered mindless with terror at the sight of a twist of seaweed. We'd be galloping along the sand in the early morning, the wind in our hair, when she'd suddenly catch sight of a bit of this horrifying substance, bound sideways with all her feet in the air, and I'd go flying off at right angles to land on the damp sand.

There is nothing so unyielding as damp sand and I can't think why I'm not dead. Following a chase towards the renowned quicksand on the approach to Conwy, I would climb back on the animal and we would make our way up the hill, through the village to the soft fields.

One of the better things about being on a horse is that you can see over hedges into people's windows. This is especially rewarding in the early evening after they've put their lights on but before they've drawn their curtains. She lived in the Graiglwyd field between the farm and our cottage, just below the mountain, and her constant wish was to get out and go and live with the mountain ponies.

Sadly they refused to accept her. Whenever she escaped – which was often – they would reject her. Teeth bared, ears laid back, they would bite her and kick her, and generally manifest hostility, while the poor thing tried to ingratiate herself with her wild relations. I didn't feel much compassion for her as I flew round the gorse bushes with a rope halter.

Once I was sitting in the Crescent cinema rapt in a film when a message flashed on the screen to the effect that she'd got away again. In the end I sold her to a man in Llandudno, who wanted a quiet mount for his daughter. Well, she was as good as gold as long as she didn't see seaweed or hear the call of the wild.

THERE WAS AN area just above Graiglwyd that seemed to have something of the spatial equivalent of eternity – just a small circle of mountainside that could have existed at any point in time and anywhere in the world. Short, dry turf, gnarled hawthorns, white with blossom in the spring and heavy with crimson berries at the end of the summer; a stream, narrow and bright and as cold as death, and shallow outcrops of rock where little snakes would bask in the sun if there were no children around. In the old days it was supposed that these *gwiberod* grew wings if they could get their fangs on some mother's milk. They would grow into huge dragons and fly over the countryside wreaking destruction, shadowing the hills and pastures and eating people.

How, one asks oneself, would a viper contrive to get itself suckled by a woman? Women have been known to suckle piglets, and there was a much admired Victorian representation of a lady extending this service to her starving grandpapa – but snakes? It has been suggested that women working in the fields, or travelling with their babies, might have expressed surplus milk on to the ground, whereupon, I suppose, vipers streaked out of their holes and lapped it up. An unconvincing hypothesis. I'm sure there were dragons in the old days, but I don't think that's how they came about. I'm more frightened of snakes than I am of dragons – this is because they've got no legs, and I'm frightened of spiders because they've got too many – but it seems to be true that snakes are quite as frightened of people as people are of them. As for dragons – the wizards and heroes and saints, long ago, exterminated them all. It is said that they ranged boldly far and wide, but I have tried to imagine cowering in a hut or a castle while a winged monster beat around the walls, and I can't.

It seems more likely that dragons would have lurked in their mountain fastnesses, kept their heads down, and confined their activities to picking off stray sheep or cattle who had wandered absent-mindedly away from the herd. Sometimes, of course, a shepherd, pilgrim or robber must have rounded a crag and come upon a cave in the curling mists, and there encountered something so blood-chilling that his beard – if there was time – went instantly white, while his crook, staff or battle-axe dropped from his nerveless fingers. I can imagine that. Up by the Jubilee path there are holes in the hill where, before the days of the Empress, uncanny things might have made their dwelling place.

But it is difficult now to evoke the Penmaenmawr of twenty years ago, let alone the Penmaenmawr of the dawn of history. All the layers of the past have been fractured and splintered together so that it is no longer recognisable; no longer a place for warring tribesmen to battle over; no longer a community of farmers, and shopkeepers and quarrymen and schoolteachers. The Edwardian air that once characterised parts of it has been dispelled, all evidence of the gentry who once frolicked there expunged. There are bungalows on the tennis courts, the Grand Hotel has changed its nature, and the largest of the villas (which was also, at one time, a home for bad boys) is now

surrounded by a caravan park. Its drive, flanked by drowsy rhododendrons, used to lead nowhere and to no one, to a silent empty house under the mountain where incongruous house-parties must have flourished with shrieks of 'Who's for tennis?' echoing in the groves where once the makers of flint axes would have wandered. The municipal gardens – like everywhere else, sloping down towards the sea – are still there but not quite what they were in the days when Mair's father fished one of my cousins out of the stream just before he was sluiced down the town drain under Pantyrafon. The tropical greenhouses are in disrepair and there is not the same floral abundance as met the eyes of the Edwardian visitors.

The Romans were there too, engaged with their *idée fixe* of making straight roads – a compulsion which seems to have bedevilled the human race intermittently throughout the centuries. I don't think they stayed in Pen. They must have wriggled round Penmaen Point in order to go on to Anglesey and exterminate the Druids. There is a rumour that these Druids roasted people alive, hung in wicker cages over glowing coals. I wondered about the feasibility of this, but I suppose if they used green willow and soaked it well the cages would hold together longer than the people.

IT ISN'T JUST the ages that wrought changes in Penmaenmawr. It changed with the seasons. In the winter its whole complexion whitened, the chapels and houses bleached by the chill salt air, the pale light. It appeared a strong, grey place, its bones showing; and the best plan was to catch a cold, persuade your mother you were in no condition to go to school and sit on the rug by the kitchen range with a bag of bull's-eyes and a book.

If it snowed you could make a remarkable recovery and go out sledging down the field, taking care to turn sharply before you slammed into the iron bedstead that formed part of the fence at the bottom of the best run. One year it snowed so much that the lanes filled up and you walked on the crest of the hedges. The sea froze too, and the adults didn't like it, but for irresponsible children the conditions were ideal.

There is a story from further inland about another occasion when snow filled the lanes. A man was going home one evening when he saw a funeral procession in the distance. He pressed aside to keep out of the way, but as it drew closer he knew it to be unreal, for the mourners and bearers were treading the air, their slowly stepping feet on a level with the hedge-tops. It was already deep winter and the next week it snowed until the lanes were full. A neighbour died and the cortège had to make its way to the graveyard walking above the hedgerows. It is not related how they managed to bury the body.

There are hundreds and hundreds of recorded instances of phantom funerals in Wales. Also of the *canwyll corff* – the candles that herald a death and glimmer around the gateways of the doomed. It is said that St David asked them of God to warn the more fractious parishioners that their time was nearly up and they should mend their ways. The *deryn corff* or *deryn y meirw*, the bird of death, is another unwelcome reminder of mortality, indeed of imminent decease. He taps at your window. I, however, have ceased to mind him for he and many of his kind spend hours hammering at ours. If they were correct in their predictions our family and most of our acquaintance would be decimated by now.

It is the crows who are the worst offenders. Their beak marks disfigure the panes, they have pecked out the putty and now they have started on the wooden frames. I caught one at it one morning just as dawn broke. I heard him clattering away and I crept downstairs, barefoot, to the room where he stood on the window sill. Then I leapt in front of him and *screamed*. I never saw a bird move so fast. He gave a squawk of the purest terror and almost turned white. I may have given him a heart attack. Vengeance is satisfying. I recently had a good idea. I'm going to paint the window frames with the hottest chilli sauce available to man.

MY LIFE CHANGED when I went to school in Bangor. I had previously seldom been further south than Llanfairfechan since our preferences lay in the direction of Conwy and the lamented Fairy Glen. Now I had to walk from the top road to the station every morning and get on the train. When it was cold the porter used to light a fire in the waiting room, since this was in the days before progress. Now there's no fire, no porter and no waiting room and the main trains don't stop there any more.

The trains then were burlier, more substantial than the effete sort we get now. The seats were covered in a patterned, carpet-like substance. There were butch docker's belt-type straps to let the windows up and down, and glazed, framed photographs of scenic wonders on the bulwarks, and the school train went through – again I quote *Welsh Pictures* – 'the most interesting and picturesque part of the coast-line of North Wales'. The station at Llanfairfechan was particularly diverting with wooden carved bees, butterflies and flowers adorning the platform.

I still dream about the stretch of land that lay to the left as the train approached Bangor – meadows and groves and stone cottages level with the sands – and the sea stretching away on the right to Anglesey and Puffin Island which was once known as Priestholm and is really called Ynys Seiriol after the saint who lived there in the sixth century – a vintage century for saints: there seem to have been hundreds of them.

When Gerald of Wales got round there it was 'inhabited by hermits, who live in the service of God by the labour of their hands. They are remarkable in that, should they have ever quarrelled with each other for reasons of human frailty, a species of small mice, which abound on the island, consume most of their food and drink and befoul the rest.' The worst thing about mice is that they have peculiar urinary arrangements and are totally incontinent, carelessly peeing wherever they happen to be, even in the midst of their lunch. The hermits are long gone and the island given over to seabirds and rats. At one time people used to pickle the eponymous puffins and eat them as a delicacy. They sound disgusting – fishy, feathery and vinegary.

Some say that Maelgwn Gwynedd is buried on Puffin Island. He, too, flourished in the sixth century and led a luxurious life in his castle above Deganwy. It is now impossible to equate Deganwy with sumptuousness but that is how times change. He was fond of music and organised an early eisteddfod in Conwy, and once held a competition with some other kings – a species of the 'chicken' game (also practised by Canute) – to see who could sit on his throne longest on the sands as the sea came in. Maelgwn had ingeniously contrived that his throne should float, so he won; nevertheless he must have presented a droll spectacle, bobbing about on the waves. So must his defeated rivals, hurrying shorewards with their thrones. I have seen the same thing happen to people who lingered too long in their deck-chairs, handkerchieves over their faces, unconscious of the creeping tide.

One day Maelgwn's nephew Elffin called on him bringing his bard – who was none other than the famed Taliesin who was also a wizard. Now, uncle and nephew had one of those ridiculous and meaningless arguments so usual in families. Each claimed that *his* wife was the most chaste in the world. It got so heated that Maelgwn flung his nephew into the dungeon, and sent off his son Rhun to test the virtue of Elffin's wife. In these enlightened days Maelgwn's wife would doubtless have been deeply offended by this public discussion of her personal life, but one gets the impression that she sat there simpering while Elffin's wife, instead of smacking Rhun's face, behaved in an egregiously convoluted and thoughtlessly unkind fashion. Having been warned to expect a person intent on seduction she dressed her maid in her own clothes and put

Elffin's ring on her finger. It wasn't made clear in the version I was told but I imagine that Rhun inveigled himself into the affections of the unfortunate girl – then, as proof, he chopped of the ring-bearing finger and bore it home. To anyone with any sense this would prove nothing but that he was a sadistic beast, but Maelgwn was delighted with the evidence.

Elffin was shown the finger and smiled scornfully. The finger was too fat for his wife's, he said. His wife cut her nails every Saturday and this nail hadn't been trimmed for a month. What's more – he said – the erstwhile owner of the finger had recently been making rye-bread, for some dough remained under the nail. His wife had never been known to bake bread in all her born days. The story concludes with the intimation that the laugh was on Rhun, but we are not told what were the feelings of the wronged and fingerless maid.

Elffin remained incarcerated, so Taliesin got him out by dumbfounding Maelgwn's bards, whose skills were the pride of the court. He read out a long poem which left them speechless, so Elffin was released and the spell was lifted – if spell it was, and not the stupefaction of boredom induced by having to listen to someone else reading aloud his work. Not content with this, Taliesin went on to prophesy the death of his master's host and uncle. A monster, he said, would emerge from Morfa Rhianedd (on the death stretch), a yellow creature – yellow all over, even to its hair and eyes and teeth – to put an end to Maelgwn Gwynedd. At this the king locked himself in the church. He walked up and down, fretting as he wondered what was going on outside; then, unable to bear the suspense, he peeped through the keyhole, saw the yellow peril and dropped dead. The rationalist holds that this monster was the yellow plague which swept through Europe at about that time, but then how did Taliesin know it was coming? After Maelgwn died the monks took him in a boat to Puffin Island. He had built them a monastery there and perhaps they felt that this would be a way of expressing their gratitude. He was not, it seems, a really bad man; merely short-tempered, and perhaps a little devious.

There is a story that St Seiriol, who also lived in the district, used to meet his friend St Cybi once a week. He always used to walk with the sun at his back and so never got tanned, whereas Cybi, walking with the sun on his face acquired a positively Mediterranean hue. As a result they were known as Seiriol the Fair and Cybi the Dark. The weather must have been better in those days. Now they might both have been known as the Wet.

AT THE TIME I was seldom musing on these matters as I was borne schoolwards. I was usually doing my homework. The accusing words 'You did this homework on the train' still ring in my ears. I can't imagine how I did. I can't write on trains now. Perhaps they ran more smoothly then.

When we arrived in Bangor clad in gym-slip, blazer and hat and lugging a leather satchel, there was frequently trouble at the barrier because somebody was bound to have forgotten her 'contract', a tiresome and elusive bit of cardboard which was housed in a small case with a plastic window but was wont to slip out. Friends who had already passed through the barrier would try to sneak their own contract through the bars to the bereft one, but the ticket collector had eyes like a hawk. You would think that, having seen us all every day for months on end, these eyes would have relayed to the brain of the collector the fact that if we had had a contract the day before it was more likely that we had mislaid it than that we were trying to defraud the railway company, but he didn't think that way.

Then came the next mile walk up a steep lane, across a field and up a short road between houses to the school gates – some of us with books still open as we strove to learn the passages of verse we should have learned the night before. There were some girls who had in fact done that, and walked holding their heads high, carefree and confident – *smug* is perhaps the word I'm groping for – but I tended not to know them well.

School was a red-brick building looking out over fields and hills, surrounded by gardens. It smelled, like all schools, of polish and chalk and dinner, and on the whole I didn't much care for it. During the first year I was one of the good girls and was made Form Captain with a little red badge to prove it, but after that I went downhill. The

place was run on public-school lines with Houses and House Captains, Prefects and a Head Girl and I never could drum up the requisite loyalty to my House (which was called Tryfan after the mountain). Sometimes a Games Captain would burst into tears if her House was beaten in a match, which I found incomprehensible, not being of a political cast of mind, and I put a lot of thought and ingenuity into getting out of games at every possible opportunity.

The hockey pitch was set on an eminence open to the winds of the sea and hills. There would be a shriek from a whistle, a cry from the Games Mistress of 'Bully off' and two huge girls would clash sticks over a ball, after which all hell broke loose with people charging about knee-deep in mud, cracking each other over the shins. My Sunday friend, Mair, once distinguished herself and won brief fame by knocking out the Head Girl with an injudicious swing of her stick, but usually the game was boring and alarming in equal parts.

Netball and tennis were plain boring and the yearly Sports Day acceptable only in so far as there weren't any lessons while it was in progress. Whenever I find myself in the middle of a large flat, short-grassed field I experience a lowering of the spirits traceable to the time when such an environment meant leaping about doing long jumps, short jumps, high jumps, and running around in relay races.

School dinner sometimes consisted of corned beef stew followed by Spotted Dick with white flour sauce, and the occasional salad consisted of cold corned beef with slices of tomato and lettuce leaves, undressed except for those small primitive forms of life, legless or too-many-legged, which habitually compete with the human race in the matter of salad.

I WENT BACK to have a look at my old school recently. It took some time finding it. I wouldn't have thought it would be difficult to locate – a bloody big red-brick building set on an eminence looking out over the Snowdon range – but could we find it? No we couldn't. We cruised around the roads seeking vainly for the institution where I had spent my formative years while I wondered if I'd gone mad and simply imagined eight years of Latin and maths and domestic science and hanging in the gym from those Spanish Inquisition-type horizontal bars like an exemplary dead mole on a farmer's fence. We passed a vast new edifice labelled Ysgol Friars, and that didn't help because the Friars' school I remembered was an old grey building – all stone and ivy. Every now and then I would recognise a landmark and squawk, 'That's where Lowri used to live' or 'That's where I nearly froze to death watching a football match', but on the whole the terrain was unfamiliar.

We had to ask directions in the end, from an old gentleman mowing the lawn outside a house that I'll swear wasn't there twenty years ago. This proved to be the problem. New houses and all manner of other new buildings had sprung up all over the place. The patch of common ground that used to open up after you left the lane from the station is now built on. No wonder I was confused. When we finally tracked down my elusive school we found unfamiliar extensions sprouting from it and loads of little girls *and* boys scuttling round. It had gone Comprehensive. The whole place is no longer called Bangor County Grammar School for Girls, but Tryfan, like my old house. No more girls in gym-slips (so unflattering to the newly developed bosom), no more red blazers, red and white ties or school hats. I shouldn't be at all surprised if the children were now allowed to run in the corridors and wear as many hair grips as they like – the girls, that is. Any of us caught moving at an unseemly pace in the corridors had to suffer detention, and mistresses were constantly scrutinising our coiffures for evidence of more than the statutory two grips. This strikes me as a daft rule, for two are not really sufficient to keep your hair out of your eyes and should you wish to put the stuff in a bun you need about a hundred. I used to have plaits, the ends of which I chewed in moments of deep concentration. My mother spent years trying to persuade the left side of my hair to curve into a 'natural wave'. All this was wasted when one day a little friend stubbed out her chewing gum in it and it had to be cut in a fringe which I have retained ever since.

Once they had developed busts a lot of the girls simultaneously took to trying to bash their school hats into more becoming shapes. Anyone apprehended not wearing her school hat whilst clad in school uniform would be severely reprimanded and, in all probability, flung into detention, and, since no one looks her best with a black felt pudding basin jammed over her ears, much millinery ingenuity was called into play with judicious dents and folds enabling the headgear to perch at what is known as a 'jaunty angle'.

The really precocious girls used to keep lipsticks in their pencil cases and apply it surreptitiously when out of sight of the school gates – an offence for which corporal punishment would not have seemed inappropriate. Any jostling or raucous behaviour in the streets, station or at the bus stop would be promptly reported to the Headmistress by the vigilant townspeople and the term here is 'Woe betide the culprit'.

Considering how much I detested school uniform it is perverse of me now to regret its passing. After my last day at school – and I may as well say now that, like all the best people, I was expelled – I threw my school hat out of the train window. I'd been planning to do that for months. You may be asking yourself why I was expelled and I have to disappoint you. It was just that school was as tired of me as I was of it. The Headmistress wearily told my mother that she didn't think they had any more to offer me, and while I think I was wonderfully well taught – and thank God and the schoolmistresses for it – I never really liked secondary school. They were not the happiest days of my life – those came later and have gone again.

I DID HAVE an interesting sensation as I strolled, on this last trip, through the main doors and knocked on the door of what is now the Head*master*'s office. Analysing it I found it to be a sense of relief that I had not been sent out of class to report myself for inattention and whispering in scripture, and I would not have to go on to struggle hopelessly with logarithms under the pink, scornful eye of Miss Reid, or shin up one of those ropes, clad in gym knickers (it seems silly to have had to take off one's gym-slip in order to do gym), or hurl myself over a 'horse' on to a scratchy mat. Even better – I need never again mend a hedge tear or make Scotch broth to be taken home in a jar, and never, never again need I eat gritty mince with waterlogged potatoes.

After I had explained the purpose of my visit – which was to refresh my memory – the two male teachers, who were very kindly putting up with me, looked enquiringly at the roll of Honour flanking the hall clock where the names of those luminous souls who had got Exhibitions and Scholarships were displayed.

'No good looking for me there,' I said, without going into details, for teachers still frighten me. (I had gone on to Liverpool School of Art which was very good for a year while most of the students were ex-servicemen, but when they left a lot of spotty ex-schoolboys arrived; quite a different kettle of fish, so I left too. Some of these boys went on to become Beatles.)

I had been accustomed to male teachers, at the national school and the art school, but it seemed strange to see them in Bangor County Grammar School for Girls where the only man had been the caretaker – morose as caretakers always are – who I remember plodding round the place with mop and bucket, scattering sawdust on sick, poor wretch.

The main hall where we used to assemble each morning for prayers and hymns was also used to stage the plays and eisteddfodau, which at least had the merit of getting you off lessons for a while. Music was an integral and genuine part of Welsh school life, rooted in tradition, culture and custom. I was no good at it, being unable, as the man said, to distinguish between 'God Save the Weasel' and 'Pop goes the King', but I saw its importance. I have since learned that – certainly in the case of ILEA – the words 'We have a very strong music department here' on the lips of a head teacher mean that the rest of the curriculum is effing useless, but it wasn't so in Bangor. To many of my peers singing came as naturally as breathing and there were constant concerts apart from the main school eisteddfod which happened on St David's Day with much brandishing of daffodils and leeks. I was permitted only to appear in a tableau as Botticelli's Flora in a frock which didn't fit, clutching a bunch of flowers and gazing winsomely into the middle distance. I felt a fool, and haven't cared for public appearances since.

However, I did once win a prize for a painting at the *National* Eisteddfod and I've got a certificate to prove it. I used to prefer the small local and school eisteddfodau to the National one. The National was too big and I found it alarming – all the booths and tents and the acres of trodden grass and mud. I used, too, to worry about the people who didn't win. The joy of the triumphant was offset by the despondency of the defeated. I never could see why they minded quite so much, but the tears of the unsuccessul competitors and their families and supporters must have contributed something to the all-pervasive damp. I found these tears more moving than the acclamations afforded to the victorious. It was also too easy to get lost in all that space and I detested getting lost. It never seemed to happen up on the mountains, but if I was taken somewhere highly populated sooner or later I would completely lose my bearings and have to be ignominiously hunted down.

The field is 'dry' in the sense of alcohol-free. I have a friend who, as a young reporter on a Cardiff newspaper, was sent to cover the events of the Eisteddfod. Traditionally few journalists are teetotal and he, with some of his fellows, contrived to smuggle some cans of beer concealed about their persons on to the field. They were apprehended by a vigilant official and thrown out. Knowing that their editors would not be happy about this they avenged themselves by informing the Gorsedd that the vigilant official was in possession of spiritous liquors.

One of the glorious drawbacks of my school was that the higher windows looked out over Tryfan, the Glyders, Elidir and Carnedd. A true lover of scenery would never have done a stroke of work.

GIVEN ITS SITUATION and its age, Bangor is strangely characterless, lacking even the appeal of the parvenu Llandudno. It has a university and a cathedral, but each seems to be standing in the place of the other – the university on a commanding height and the cathedral slumped down in the centre of town. It has Penrhyn Castle which was built in the nineteenth century and therefore lacks historical interest except for the Penrhyn Lock-outs, which happened around the turn of the century and left a bitter, black memory.

The Lord Penrhyn of the time, who owned the slate quarries around Bethesda, refused to negotiate with the quarrymen's union and the community was divided into those who went along with Lord Penrhyn and those who didn't. Many left to look for work elsewhere and those who remained had to have police protection on the way to and from the quarries. The bad feeling lingered for years and the slate industry was never the same again. At one time there was so much slate it was even used for fencing – tall slabs wired together.

We used to be taken on school trips to Blaenau Ffestiniog to watch the workers splitting slate – an extraordinarily skilled and hazardous task. It was rumoured that a flying slate could sever your jugular or take your head off.

The diversion on the way home was to try and count as many pubs and chapels as you could. I cannot now remember what the score was, but the number of both was remarkable.

Bangor also has a pier which I find it difficult to imagine thronged with holidaymakers. Perhaps the very featurelessness is a form of protective colouring to

discourage the tourist. If you are not a student or a commercial traveller there seems little reason to call in at Bangor.

One of the more thrilling aspects of my girlhood was the dancing lessons held on the training ship, the *Conway*, which was moored in the Straits opposite Plas Newydd where the Marquess of Anglesey lives. I had been forced, when I was six or so, to go to the dancing classes offered by Mrs Wynn, the doctor's wife, and had found the whole business utterly detestable. Leaping about in the back row of the chorus, clad in a blouse made from a redundant parachute and pants made from blackout material while Miss Parry hammered out a song called 'I love to climb an apple tree' on the piano, did not fully cohere with the rather virile image I held of myself at that time. I would have preferred to be out with the war-party on the foothills.

Ten years later, dancing lessons took a different form – the waltz, the foxtrot, the tango – and at least had the merit of some point. If you went to dances it was convenient to be able to dance, whereas ballet and tap-dancing were of no practical use whatsoever.

It had been decided that the cadets on the *Conway* should acquire these skills as well as navigation, holystoning decks, lugging the mainsail, learning how to cook the cabin boy should the need arise, and whatever else they did, and the girls' grammar school presented a handy source of partners.

We were rowed out to the ship in little boats in the evenings with the sun setting and the wind rising over the water. It was a ship of the time of Nelson and an artefact of unbelievable beauty. One day they decided to move it and the tow rope broke, so it drifted on to the shore under the Menai Bridge and died.

Before this calamity happened I once got into terrible trouble for missing the liberty boat and spending the evening sitting under a rhododendron with a particularly charming cadet who must have missed it too. I don't remember the details. We behaved with perfect decorum, but nobody believed us and a ridiculous fuss ensued. I used to feel sorry for the Friars' school boys who went around in school uniform. They could not compete with the glamour of the naval attire of the *Conway* cadets and must have found it galling.

WHEN I WAS very young I used to go as a really special treat to Anglesey with a local tradesman known simply as Uncle Roberts. We would quarter the island in his old van, going from one remote farmhouse to another. Looking back I think these must have been smuggling forays, for rationing was in force and while he certainly bought a lot of apples and plums – perfectly legal apparently – he also bought farm butter and chickens which were contraband and were thus carefully secreted underneath piles of the more innocuous purchases. I imagine I was taken along as cover; a child and a gentle old man do not fit the picture of the cut-throat desperadoes who habitually engage in this trade. The van was searched at least once by whoever was responsible for stamping out the butter and chicken traffic, for I remember the expression of innocence on the face of Uncle Roberts as he indicated his boxes of plums, standing at the back of the van – being too old and frail to unpack the lot – and anyway wasn't it time the child was in bed? Only a brute would have persevered with his investigations.

I remember the island as wild – not, of course, as wild as it must have been when the Druids held sway, although I suspect that, as is usual with conquerors, the Romans gave them a needlessly bad press. From the little we know – for it seems the Druids were averse to writing things down – it appears that they were monotheistic and had a fairly sophisticated system of hierarchy. It is quite possible that they didn't burn people in baskets but led a peaceful existence devoted to art and the state of the crops until the ghastly Romans came along and ruined it all. When the Romans left, the island settled down again and the people devoted themselves mainly to the blameless occupations of farming and fishing.

We would lurch through lanes and cart-tracks hung with age-old hedges and come to farmyards where the dogs would snarl, cower or curtsey at our feet, according to temperament.

There were then few *improvements* in the farmhouses with their wooden dressers and settles, the blacked iron range and the shining slate floors. In the dairies the butter was kept in slate drawers, and there was a sense of the almost religious cleanliness that comes from simplicity and hard work: the absence of unnecessary embellishment, of

cloth – curtains, chair-covers, rugs and cushions. Uncle Roberts said that some of the women had to walk two or more miles daily to fetch water and it wasn't an easy life – but it *was* life, with centuries of purpose and tradition behind it. Everyone, you felt, knew what he was for. Some of the people spoke only Welsh and never left the island, and some of them left to become academics and politicians and singers and all manner of things. Who, I would ask, is that man in the orchard? 'That's my brother, the Regius Professor of Greek.'

You may be saying to yourself that this is what happens everywhere, but it isn't – not in the same way. There is a feeling now that change is not only inevitable but desirable and that everyone must work to 'better himself'. This arises from the consciousness of a class-ridden society, which Wales was not. It has its grandees, but on the whole their history is their own and separate from the recent history of the mass of the people. What I think I'm trying to say is this: if a way of life is fulfilling, the fact that your parents, grandparents and great-grandparents lived in the same way back to the time when the Romans called it a day and took the boat home is no reason to be pleased when you are forced to alter it. To be fair, one nobleman who visited the island in 1755 described it as

> a neglected unpleasant county, without a tree or a hedge to be seen in it and cultivated so ill from the obstinacy of the people in adhering to the ignorance of their forefathers that I am told [I wonder who told him?] it does not produce the tenth part of what the land would be capable if improved by the agriculture of England.

This does not agree with the view that Anglesey was known as Môn and described as the Mother of Wales because she could grow enough grain to sustain the whole of the rest of the Principality. These eighteenth-century tourists in Wales seem to have been invariably dissatisfied and always complaining. They all grumbled and fussed incessantly. They didn't like the food, they didn't like the inns, they didn't like the mountains; they hated the whole journey and they must have been hell to travel with. One wonders why they bothered. (And how ill they compare with Giraldus, who, even if he took a somewhat credulous interest in all that he saw, remained alert and appreciative.) The miserable old parties of the eighteenth century sound very much like the worst kind of child being taken on holiday. 'Mummy, Mummy, when are we going to *get* there?' 'Urghh, I can't eat *this*.' 'Why is that lady wearing that funny hat?' 'I feel sick,' etc. etc. What these travellers mean is that they much prefer their own backyard, to which they are accustomed, and anything different is highly suspect.

As to the changes in the way of life, economic pressures, market forces and all sorts of imponderables I don't understand crowd in from outside to distort and obliterate not only the worst but the best of all that has gone before, and nothing will convince me that this is a Good Thing.

There are high-rise blocks on the shores of Anglesey. Who let them do that? And why?

LAST TIME I went there the day started fine, and then, perhaps symbolically, there descended a great Celtic mist. I peered through it looking for the pink-washed cottages of my memory, but they'd gone. All over Wales hundreds and hundreds of the old stone cottages have fallen down and in their place have appeared 'Dunroamin' – suburban bungalows with geraniums and lobelias in flower baskets, pointless balconies of meanly-wrought iron, two-tone cladding and picture windows, and little lawns so that the middle-aged people can mow them and feel close to the earth, claiming their territory with pokerwork signs announcing 'Dunroamin'. And, of course, there are always the housing estates – living graveyards. Even when the stone-built cottages have been bought up they have frequently been Englished with bottle-bottom windows and carriage lamps, and the dreadful homogenisation that is creeping all over the Isles of Britain is creeping even into the wildernesses.

In 1908 two Welsh architects wrote a book called *The Old Cottages of Snowdonia*. They said:

> Now it has been wisely ordained that the loftier and grander parts of our mountain scenery should not as a rule be habitable, otherwise the awe these majestic masterpieces of nature rightly demand might be diminished. It is well that these great mountain peaks should remain apart from all human habitation to give us an opportunity amid the vast and solitary surroundings of being impressed to the full with their wild grandeur.
>
> Along the seacoast and in the valleys, however, the case is different. There the mountains form indeed an impressive, but not an awe-inspiring background, and

we live as it were at a level not too exalted to be associated with cheerfulness of mind and domestic happiness. It is there that we find the little farmsteads, each with its old cottage in the centre of a few small fields carefully walled in; and we cannot but feel that even if these humble dwellings were more numerous than they are, their white walls and lowly purple roofs could but give that animated touch and suggestion of human interest that would be lacking in a scene otherwise perfect. They do not detract but rather add to the beauty of the picture of which they form so integral a part.

The old buildings, however, may be studied not only from an *artistic* but also from an *historical* point of view; for just as the many-branched Welsh oaks are peculiar to the Principality, so are these buildings the natural product of the country, the tree growth as it were of the soil, and show as clearly as any written history the development of the life of the people. Not only is it essential, if we would preserve the marvellous beauty of our country – the greatest treasure we possess – that we should understand these traditional methods of building, so completely in harmony with it, but also, if we would understand rightly the past, there is no better book for us to study than the old homes of our ancestors.

Sad to relate, most of these ancient structures are in the last stages of decay, and therefore in a few years' time these valuable pages of national history and native building will be lost forever. It is earnestly to be hoped that greater interest may be taken in them before it is too late.

Too late. Eighty years later over miles of countryside you will pass ruin after ruin, growing depressed and hopeless until you reach 'Dunroamin' again, when you begin to feel ill and reflect that death won't be so bad if it takes you beyond the reaches of suburbia. Perhaps the loss of the vernacular is as important in regard to the indigenous architecture as it is to the language. I don't know where suburbia should rightly begin and end, or even why the very concept is so lowering to the spirits, but it should not extend into the wildness of the country.

We came to an aspect of Anglesey that I recognised: a stretch of age-old untidiness, of topsy-turvy field, ancient rocks and untrimmed hedgerow (according to Hooker's

hypothesis very ancient hedgerow, so I don't know where our nobleman was looking) and I was relieved until we rounded a corner and there was 'Dunroamin' again, smirking through its branches of ornamental cherry. Down to the shore where the ghosts of mermen might have lingered just beyond the mist – and then to the left where there were another couple of bungalows.

Then there are the marinas. It was some time before I realised that boats can be as suburban as bungalows. When I thought of boats I thought of wooden fishing vessels or the mucky old hulks that used to take away the granite and slate from the quarries. I knew there were such things as pleasure craft, but I gave them no thought until one day I realised that there were so many in Conwy harbour that you could have walked over them to the fishing grounds. These boats are moulded out of fibreglass and, grouped together, are no more than a water-borne caravan park. The people who sail about in them are, I believe, under the impression that by doing so they are coming close to the elemental force of the ocean.

The same thing is happening in, amongst other places – perhaps *most* other places – Celtic Brittany. The approach to Quiberon is littered with brand-new villas standing cheek by jowl and when you get there the harbour is packed with plastic boats. If the trend continues, all the citizens of the developed nations will spend half their time touring each other's countries, and very soon all those countries will be indistinguishable one from another; whereupon, I suppose, we will all stay at home bemoaning the deathly boredom of our surroundings.

When a country becomes dependent on tourism for its economic survival its spirit is as good as dead. The appearance of vitality is spurious, as in a carcase overrun by maggots.

I was going to say that I don't really think of the poor tourist as a maggot, but on consideration I find that I do. The tourist of today does not whine to the extent that he would have done in the eighteenth century, but this is only because he has prevailed upon the places he visits to resemble in many respects the place he has come from, and so he feels at home with his fish and chips, his Chinese take-away, the knick-knacks in the tourist shops, and the boat he built from a kit in his back garden.

ONE OF MY school friends used to live in Beaumaris, in a house opposite the castle, which was considered in its time to be impregnable. As it was apparently never completely finished one wonders how this could be, but it seems it was very craftily designed with a moat and inner and outer walls. It was assumed, I suppose, that assailants, having negotiated the moat (which was doubtless full of sewage), and stormed the outer walls, would be discouraged on finding themselves under the inner walls, while the beleaguered inhabitants poured boiling oil on them. As the inner walls

were higher than the outer it should have been apparent to the invaders that they were likely to have a problem, but perhaps their generals, leading from the rear, forced them on with screams and threats.

The castle is now so peaceful, surrounded by greensward and teashops, that I found it impossible to imagine a battle raging there. I tried because the young have little sense of the realities of bloodshed, and old warfare seemed exciting. Now I think how inconvenient it must have been for the civilian living in a battle-torn land; how alarming for the soldier to find himself confronted by an enraged opponent, bristling

with weapons and intent on killing. In one way I find that I do not regret the past.

The winding road to Beaumaris was flanked by rhododendrons and the tropical plants which are commonly attributed to the nearness of the Gulf Stream – rather as people in Chelsea, some years ago, who were in doubt about their parentage, laid claim to Augustus John as their father. It was another magical stretch but strangely un-Welsh. I think the Edwardians must have got at it and planted those foreign trees. Beaumaris, like Conwy and Caernarfon was, once, reserved for English gentry, while the Welsh were allowed in from the surrounding countryside only on market days.

One of these gentlefolk, Sir Richard Bulkeley, met an unfortunate fate at the hands of his wife and one Sir Thomas Cheadle, a bad egg. I read the account of this matter years ago in an old copy of *The Anglesey Transactions* which I can't find, so I'm a little vague about the details – which is perhaps just as well since there were quoted many contemporary forensic tit-bits which would put you off your dinner. Sir Thomas was the son of a swineherd who had been promoted to steward. He kicked off in life as a pirate and ended up in the 'Deputie Constableshipp of Bewmares'. (Mind you, it was also suggested that Sir Richard was a pirate. Perhaps everyone was a pirate.) He fell for the wife of Sir Richard, and together – so it is alleged, as they say in legal circles – they conspired to poison him. It took some time. Arsenic was, in all likelihood, the substance chosen and its effects were unpleasant indeed (this is where the details come in). Suffice it to say that Sir Richard slowly expired.

Sir Thomas then married the widow, and now it gets very complicated. I have rediscovered my *Transactions*, but it doesn't really help since the whole episode is almost impossible to follow. Lady Anne, the widow, disowned two of her children by Sir Richard and said they were the children of her maid Bessie. I don't know why, but I expect Sir Thomas put her up to it. They went to court to try and prove that they *were* her children, while her son Richard tried to prove that his mother and stepfather had poisoned his father. Lady Anne then grew hoity-toity and wrote letters reproving him for being mean to his mother. She also took a high tone about the accusation of poisoning and said loftily that if Sir Thomas was to be blamed for this she too wished to share in his tribulations.

They were eventually (I think wrongly) acquitted, but then Sir Thomas got himself into more deep water, for 'in the year 1645-6 hee began to practice disloyaltie, writing two letters in the same Morning, one to the Lord Byron Generall for the King professing all Loyaltie, the other to Thomas Mytton Esq: Generall for the Parliament, to proffer the delivery of his castle of Lleniog into the hands of the Parliament-forces'. These letters were intercepted, thereby 'betreying his Legerdemayne', so 'his person was imprisoned and not released until the whole Island of Anglisey was yeelded to the Parliament AD 1646'.

Cheadle's luck had definitely run out, for when the Island revolted against Parliament 'againe' in 1648 the Royalists slung him into prison in the Castle of Beaumaris. 'Hereafter Cheadle began to decay in his Intellectuals; and grewe sottish, nasty and very frindlesse.' He was done for debt and Lady Anne, who had gone off him by now, refused to put up bail. 'And when hee was released out of prison, his Lady could not abide his nastinesse, being unable to retayne either Ordwe or Urine. Att last being removed to a house of a Neece of his neare Tal Y Cafn in Caernavonshire, hee died in great misery full of diseases as the Diarrhoea, Mictus involuntarius, Herodian-disease etc.'

Lady Anne fared little better, surviving him by several years, but suffering from the stone and gravel. 'In a fitt shee would crie out: In good Earnest I find now the greatest payne where I formerly found the greatest pleasure.' It seems that she never showed any repentance for her wicked life but rather 'gloryed in her shame', and thus ends another great love story.

Some years later a different Richard Bulkeley was riding over the Lavan Sands towards Penmaenmawr (the death stretch) when he met the son of Sir Thomas, Major Richard Cheadle. Words passed – I daresay Sir Richard tactlessly pointed out that the Major's papa had been a pirate and a poisoner – and Cheadle ran him through with the workmanlike sword he was carrying (Sir Richard 'having onely a short bawble of a sword').

Cheadle then took off for the mainland, leaving his wife on the sands (there is no record of what she thought about this), and went into hiding. He was finally apprehended in bed in an inn and taken to be locked up in various castles until he came before the Sessions at Conwy. As often happens with criminals he couldn't keep his mouth shut and boasted to the men who arrested him that he had been planning to kill Sir Richard for years but hadn't previously had the chance. He was found guilty, reprieved for a while and finally hanged in Conwy despite the attempts of his friends to rescue him. Apparently that was not his first murder, so he was no great loss. One wonders that such villains so often have friends. Perhaps his wickedness had extended to theft and only he knew where the booty was concealed.

A MUCH SADDER case was that of Richard Rowlands who was convicted of the murder of his father-in-law. He absolutely insisted that he was innocent and when – as the French say – 'the time came for him to be brave' he resolutely refused and barricaded himself in his cell with his bench. The governor of Beaumaris Gaol, officers and minister stood round outside reasoning with him, but he wouldn't come out. In the end they battered down the door and dragged him, protesting, to the ramp and gibbet which overlooked the street and the gaping populace. As a final gesture he cursed the church clock, saying that, in proof of his innocence, it would never go properly again. It didn't. Later another man confessed to the crime, but it was too late then for apologies.

Beaumaris Gaol is actually rather nice; not comfortable certainly, but prisoners had their own cells and it contrasts well with prevailing prison conditions today. There was a treadmill for male prisoners, admittedly, but when you think of the things to which people willingly submit themselves now in pursuit of health – exercise bikes, jogging, etc. – it doesn't seem all that barbarous. The female prisoners worked in the laundry, and there were holes in the ceiling through which hung ropes attached to the cradles on the floor above so they could rock their babies while they rinsed out the homespun. The gaol was seldom filled to capacity and is now a kind of museum, open to the unconvicted and offering a diverting few hours to the family outing.

Another interesting person died in Beaumaris on 30 November 1793. He was William Lewis of Llandisman who passed out as he was drinking a quart of Welsh ale from a cup called a *tumbler mawr*. Every morning he read so many chapters of the Bible and every evening he drank eight gallons of ale. It was calculated that, all in all, during his lifetime he must have drunk enough to float a 74-gun ship. At the time of his death he weighed forty stone and they had to construct a crane to hoick him out of his parlour and take it to the churchyard to lower him into his grave. He had called himself the King of Spain and his children were known as prince, infanta, etc. I cannot begin to imagine why, but I wish I had known him. The most remarkable thing about the present inhabitants is that most of them seem to have broken their necks. Last time I was there we counted dozens of people wearing surgical collars.

THE FIRST TIME I ever got drunk was at a hunt ball at the Bulkeley Arms. I didn't fall over, but when I got home I found I could neither lie down nor sit up with any comfort, for my head kept going round and round. Perhaps this is what prejudiced me against hunting; or it may have been the custom of throwing hot pennies from the balcony to the peasantry below – an ill-conceived notion, I would have thought, the sort of thing the peasantry might brood over until the revolution came.

I went beagling only once, and then only because a friend insisted it would be fun. It wasn't. It was cold and I somehow got stuck with a dog called Venus, who had to be lifted over fences. It felt as though we'd covered Anglesey twice when the time came to pack it in. They caught a hare, but luckily Venus and I were hopelessly lost by then and did not witness the slaughter. I begin to think that leisure activities do not become the human race, whether chasing things with a view to killing them, or sailing about in a fibreglass boat. Why don't they read or play the piano? Harmless pastimes if you keep the window shut in the latter case – this also mutes the noise of next door's lawn-mower.

Beaumaris, however, remains comparatively unspoiled and peaceful. The blood that flooded the streets in the civil war has long since sunk into the ground. During these hostilities the Royalists barricaded themselves in the castle under the directions of yet another Bulkeley, but had to come out again because the Parliamentarian General Mytton had had the foresight to take a number of hostages and was making threatening noises. So much for the impregnability of this stronghold with its inner and outer walls and its moat. Military architects seem to have been no more clear-headed than the designers of, say, London's South Bank. Still, the castle has at least the merit of looking beautiful even in ruin, which will not be the case as the works of today's architects decay. One cavalier enthusiast, enraged at this meek surrender, impetuously leapt on his horse and rode the poor beast over a cliff. Lord knows what he thought would be gained by this large gesture. After all, he who fights and runs away lives to fight another day – if he keeps away from the cliff edge – but perhaps he was depressed. I wonder if the surviving soldiers shook their heads in puzzlement and said he'd seemed perfectly normal the day before – looking forward to the battle and making plans for the future.

A TOWN WITH a totally different ambience is Llandudno, where once I was accosted by an elderly man (he must have been about thirty) who invited me to his sailing club for a drink. I was only sixteen but I knew all about the white slave trade and declined. Often I would stand on Beaumaris shore in sunlight, looking across at Penmaenmawr menaced by rain clouds, while further on Great Ormes Head also lay in sunlight. Beyond it is Rhyl, which was rumoured by its admirers to have the greatest concentration of sun on the coast. This may be so, but we seldom went as far, since we found little of appeal in either Rhyl or Colwyn Bay. Many other people do, I hasten to add: many, many other people, as is proved by the density of humankind in the summer season. Llandudno has a greater charm.

Where it is now situated was, until quite recently, meadow and marshland with a few farms, cottages and chapels. Then along came the Victorians, bursting with energy, who flung up an entire holiday centre with hotels along the front, villas, theatres, shops, a pier and a little tramway to take the bewhiskered and crinolined revellers on trips round the Great Orme. I don't know how they did it but they managed to imbue the place with a kind of magic, a certain *chic*.

Llandudno was not shoddy. It had a style which might not, I submit, have seduced the high-born Southerner, but was perfectly adapted to the tastes of the wealthy Northerners – cotton-brokers, ship- and mill-owners, who colonised North Wales and the Lakes in search of relaxation and diversion. Contrary to southern belief, these people were not necessarily crass and brassy, but often took a far greater interest in the arts and in nature than their southern neighbours, endowing libraries and concert halls and galleries and exerting a beneficial influence over great areas. This is irrelevant, but I like to restate it whenever the opportunity arises. The Welsh too, who have a genuine and ancient culture, have been perceived as savage and backward by the insular English, who have lost theirs. It is very annoying.

The place is named after St Tudno, one of the myriad sixth-century saints, and on Great Ormes Head is what can only be described as a rocking rock which is said to be his cradle – *crud Tudno*. He, however, is not much in evidence. This is a holiday town and therefore takes little account of holy days or similar matters. I do not wish to imply that here we have Sodom or Gomorrah – there are some fine churches in the town apart from the one on the Great Orme – merely that for a sense of the numinous, of the age-old relationship between God and man, you need to go to the lonely places where men from time immemorial worshipped strange gods, until all the indefatigable saints came and baptised those sacred places, making them holy. I hope that's clear. There is something indescribably suggestive of God about parts of Wales, but it is impossible to put it into words, so I will return to the streets of Llandudno.

WHEN A NEW garment was needed for a particular occasion, such as Easter, it was to Llandudno that we went to get it. There were many dress shops but the only one I remember the name of was Marie et Cie. I had a blue dress of heavy cotton and one of cream linen with flowers embroidered on the breast; I had a blue, belted coat and skirt of woollen jersey, a grey tweed coat and skirt I could hardly walk in – but it was so *smart* – and a yellow frock with a light woollen edge-to-edge green coat to go over it.

I must have had some other clothes, but those were my favourites. Oh, and a very beautiful grey fitted woollen dress with a swishing fan of pleats behind. Never since have I worn anything so becoming. Most of the time I went round in shorts, slacks or jodhpurs and a black silk shirt somebody had looted off a dead German, but when we dressed up we put our hearts into it. The only snag was that whenever I went out in the yellow frock I came back totally obscured by greenfly.

You may find this dissertation on dress boring, but I have found that if you wish to remember the past it helps to remember what you were wearing. It must be rather like trying to remember past lives. If, perchance, we are reincarnated, we wouldn't recall much of any interest if we couldn't remember what manner of body we were clad in. Would we?

High-soled sandals and canvas sling-backs were what I preferred to put on my feet, but if I was shopping with my aunt she made me buy neat leather shoes with lowish heels and laces to go with the tailored winter wear. This aunt, Gwen, one of the seven

Griffiths girls, had married a Northerner and had come with my Uncle Johnny during the war to live in Llandudno in reduced circumstances – that is, having lost everything when the bottom fell out of their world, they had retained only the silver, the sideboard to keep it in and the cruet to sit on top with the essential bottle of Worcestershire sauce. She used to cook dainty little meals of grilled plaice with nearly transparent bread and butter, or mince with triangular snippets of toast, followed by stewed apricots. The very genteelness already had a period charm and they lived like that because they had no children.

Aunt Gwen kept her underclothes and woollens folded in tissue paper and when she went out wore a camel-hair coat, a felt pork-pie hat with a tiny feather in it, and long, long scarves of brown silk; very little and very discreet jewellery and no scent but for a little cologne. She, her mother-in-law and sisters-in-law will remain for ever in my mind as the acme of elegance: especially one known as Girly – and Olwen who got divorced, lost a fortune betting and preferred to drink in the sailors' pubs in the spit-and-sawdust bit. The rest of the family didn't much approve of her, but she didn't care.

It was my Uncle Johnny, though, who was the adult of whose company I could not get enough. He made me laugh, being the wittiest man I ever knew. And now he's dead and I can't remember the things he said. We used to walk to the West Shore and he would stop for a pint of bitter on the way back and if one of his brothers or his nephew was there too they'd bet on which gull was going to take off or whether the next dog they met would be black or brown. At home they'd lay bets on the drops of rain on the window pane.

I don't know why I found them so enchanting, but I did. It was usually in the winter that I went to stay with them, the summer being taken up with flying around on *ffrith*, and Llandudno then being too full of visitors riding donkeys and watching Punch and Judy. I never could abide the seaside in the summer, but how delightful it was with the deserted sands and the cold, grey winds and Uncle Johnny hanging on to his hat as we walked along the West Shore. (He always wore a hat in case he met a lady, whereupon he would doff it.)

It is said that Lewis Carroll met Alice Liddell when she was staying in Llandudno with her family – there is a memorial to the White Rabbit there – but I'd back my Uncle Johnny against Dodgson in the entertainment stakes any day. *Alice in Wonderland* made me suicidal when I first read it – probably one wet Sunday. It has an open-ended, uncertain quality which makes it unsuitable for those not of the soundest mind, and little children should not be subjected to it. If my mam had permitted Lewis Carroll to take me for a walk I believe I should now consider it remiss of her. The Brothers Grimm also should not be read on wet Sundays in the fastnesses of Wales. I used to find the *Girls' Crystal* far more reassuring. That world of myth and half-dream is disturbing and potentially dangerous; it is where the mad habitually wander.

On Sundays we went to Mass, for these were my Roman Catholic relations, and when I grew up I too reverted to the old religion.

LLANDUDNO IS NO longer as elegant as it was – but then nowhere is. Men with Samsonite briefcases and an implacable determination to make a great deal of money by spreading hypermarkets and franchises from coast to coast have seen to that. The smartest dress shops are now to be found in places like Chester and Shrewsbury, while Llandudno displays racks of holiday wear and crimplene skirts out on the street. In the shop windows hang draped and pleated garments in pastel shades, suitable for weddings, with hats to match. As marriage itself has gone largely out of fashion, I don't know what a sociologist or demographer would make of this. There must be a demand for these pink and lilac frocks or the shop owners would all have gone bankrupt. Elsewhere shops mostly purvey clothing for minxes – black skirts which are little more than peplums, leggings, exiguous things barely to conceal the bust and discoloured jeans with big holes in them – not clothes for brides and wedding guests.

A few weeks ago, seeking vainly for the posh tea shop which used to be approached by a narrow flight of stairs from street level, I settled for a cup of hot chocolate in an inferior establishment with Formica-topped tables bearing plastic tomatoes containing sauce. What was my astonishment to be greeted at the open door by what can only be described as a 'businesswoman' who enquired in an authoritative tone how many I was and directed me to an empty table (there were plenty). There used to be a frock-shop owner who, if you paused for a moment outside her door, would leap out and seize you, hustling you inside and forcibly trying things on you. I think they must be related. Perhaps tradition is not entirely dead.

Once when I was a girl I went with Mair to a variety show in a theatre by the sea. One of the turns consisted of a dance performed by a lady and gentleman and part of this dance necessitated the gentleman catching the lady as she did a sort of graceful, swooning back bend. He missed and the look on the lady's face as she picked herself up still causes my blood to run cold. I could barely imagine the scene in the dressing room when the performance was over but I would not have given much for the gentleman's chances of survival.

I couldn't find the street where the buses used to stop to take us home – or rather I think I may have done but the buses don't stop there any more. They probably stop, if they stop at all, on the outskirts of town to ease the congestion in the streets. My cousin Primrose once had a shocking experience on the Llandudno bus. She was coming from Penmaenmawr with her baby when he threw up in the brim of the hat of the lady in front. Primrose, aflame with embarrassment and vicarious sympathy for the unfortunate woman, promptly got off the bus by the Iron Bridge on the death stretch and waited hours in the thin salt wind for the next one.

ONCE UPON A time a traveller on the train stuck his head out of the window and the Iron Bridge knocked it off. A German plane once shed its bomb not a mile further on, demolishing a small café, and an American plane hit Foel Lûs in the mist and fell in fragments on the sands. And once, when I was very young, a private plane made the same error, and we all – the whole village – made morbid trips to gaze at it. The pilot's trousers, for some reason I could never fathom, hung on the wrecked fuselage. Perhaps they were his spare ones. There is a story that as the American plane flew to its destruction an old shepherd, seeing the red white and blue emblazoned on it,

thought it the risen phantoms of the dedicated winnowing women and hid in a hole for some time, gibbering with fright.

I should have mentioned before that one year the Irish Mail crashed on the death stretch – just by Penmaenmawr Station – with much loss of life. I didn't mention it before because I couldn't remember the date, but I don't suppose it matters. The signalman went round for weeks wearing the air of Cain and we tried not to look because we felt so sorry for him, but I think in the end he was exonerated from blame. A pushy reporter followed me home to my cousin's house saying he wished to borrow a typewriter and telephone, and my Grandpapa Griffiths, who also lived there, roared out and wiped the floor with him, not caring for the cut of his jib.

Before we left our cottage this Grandpapa used to walk along the top road to have lunch with us on Mondays – cold lamb, mashed potatoes and chutney, followed by stewed rhubarb. I distinctly remember that he gave me tobacco to chew, but that can't be right. I have absolutely no faith in history since my memory of my own is so vague, conflicting and confused. I sometimes think that at some point the young girl was simply replaced by a completely new transplant and was taken into the earth under the gnarled hawthorns and the rocky outcrops. She had no interest in babies or in cooking, she had no concept of fear and couldn't understand what her mother meant by 'worry', she bit a neighbour's child in the leg, she argued with the scripture mistress that Christ was unlikely to have been a real historical figure; on Friday nights her hair was tied in rags to make it curl and if it wasn't for remembering the clothes she wore I would doubt that she ever existed.

T HE NEW PERSON, when she was twenty-three, married a man of Welsh appearance – small and dark – and had four sons by the time she was thirty, and a son and two daughters thereafter. (And here we will pause as I do a swift contortion to get back into the first person. In the meantime I will offer a short dissertation on the history of the Welsh.)

The Welsh tend to be small and dark, descended – so it has been alleged and subsequently, I believe, disproved – from people of Iberian stock who migrated from Asia when the world was young. I have just read in a book of 1903 that the primeval population belonged to what is called the Hamitic stock represented by ancient Egyptian and modern Berber, and that many words common to Welsh and Hebrew are borrowed from the Tongue of the Hamitic people.

This interests me strangely, for I went to Egypt a few years ago and people kept saying to me, 'If you're Welsh you're going to enjoy this soup' (pressing upon me a green liquid the ingredients of which I could not begin to recognise), or, 'Well, if you're Welsh you will like this monument.' I couldn't think what they were talking about, but then I began to discern similarities between Welsh and Egyptian in the family structures, the most marked being the vast preponderance of aunties common to both peoples.

When I came home I read about a 'new' theory that the Welsh and the Berbers share the same blood group to an unusual degree. And death. The Welsh – or their ancestors, whoever they may have been – and the ancient Egyptians felt the same way about death. The master idea in both their religions was the cult of ancestors, and the menhir and the obelisk have much in common. The dolmen, the burial mound, expresses the same concern with the afterlife as the tombs in the Valley of the Kings. (This account is probably now quite out of date, as historians keep moving the goal posts.)

We spent our honeymoon in the Pen-y-Gwryd Hotel on the Llanberis Pass, a hotel designed not for honeymooners but for mountaineers, for from its doors you can make straight up the mountain paths towards Snowdon, the Glyders, Siabod, Crib-Goch and Y Lliwedd. We didn't do any of that but walked around on the flatter, boggier parts in a damp and all-pervading mist since it was a maddeningly mild December. Not as warm

as our recent Decembers have been, admittedly, but warm enough – and damp – so that you never could make up your mind what it would be correct to wear, and my smart, tweedy black frock with the shawl collar stayed on its coathanger. As did the backless black linen evening dress, because you feel a fool up in the hills in a thing more suitable to an evening at the Savoy. I only took it because my mother made me. She was thinking *honeymoon* rather than Llanberis Pass where all you really need are pants and sweaters and a great deal of waterproof wear.

Snowdonia is as subject to moods as a manic-depressive and we were unlucky to catch it on the downside. In a hard winter with the snow lying and the skies clear the mountains have the arrogant, ecstatic, dangerous air of high mania. There is nothing so intoxicating. But when the thin mountain rain drifts over every peak and pervades every gully – grey and chill and insidious – you feel you might as well hang yourself. There is no getting away from Welsh rain. It can come down vertically or it can come down horizontally. It seems to be able to come down at any angle it pleases, including upwards, for it not only goes down your neck but up your sleeves and your trouser legs. And when you go indoors it does its damnedest to follow you. You can watch it coming from a great distance, either packed up in rolling clouds or loose, blowing like a lost veil over the slopes and through the trees. It has many modes of approach and will sometimes just drop straight down on you without warning. It has been known to do that out of a clear blue sky. We spent much of our honeymoon in the bar.

A S TIME PASSED we went by train to Penmaenmawr for all our holidays. The train still stopped there then, but by now my mother lived in another cottage whose garden backed on to that of the Franciscan Friary (in the Church of which we had been married). Father Hugh, who had been our great friend when I was small, had died and I knew none of the Friars. Four little boys are rather like hamsters – however you try to cage them they get out – the road from the Sychnant Pass was near and dangerous and I didn't want them burrowing through the rowan, honeysuckle and bramble into the Friary grounds to annoy the good brothers. So we took a cottage sixty-odd miles away near Bala in the Aber Hirnant forest: a place called Ystrad y Groes, always known locally as Stacros, where I lived with the children for much of the year.

Ystrad means a flat bit of land such as you find at the bottom of a river valley, and the cottage was set amongst old meadows high on a hill where the stream curved round it. There was no other habitation for miles, no electricity and no telephone. The water came, when it came at all, from the stream further up the mountain, carried by a pipe

which the farmer's cows kept unearthing and treading on. There was an old boiler in the back kitchen which was loth to go at all and when it did boiled the water in the tank until it nearly blew up. Hearing ominous simmering noises in the night you had to leap out of bed and turn all the taps on, filling the place with steam.

The previous occupant, an Oxford don, with the impracticability of his kind, had had this system installed together with a bath, wash basin and lavatory. These, while undeniably useful when they worked, had been put in what would otherwise have been the largest bedroom and was something of a waste of space. We, however, could not afford to do anything about it, so things stayed that way. In the sitting-room, or parlour as we referred to it, there was a small iron range which in its day (about 100 years ago) had represented the height of modern technology, with a tank for heating water and a tap on one side and an oven on the other. Neither of these worked properly any longer, but the fire in the middle was our only source of heat.

That worked perfectly except when the crows built their nest in the chimney. Often, when, in our absence, they were doing this, they missed their footing and fell down it, to expire on the floor after having flown round all the rooms beating their soot-laden wings on the whitewashed walls in panic.

There was a small scullery with a sink and a larder which the don had filled with empty sherry bottles. There was also a 'dining-room' of such dampness that the desk he had left there just fell apart, its glue melted by the pervading wetness.

Stacros was altogether the dampest house I have ever known. My mother used to enquire anxiously if I had aired the beds, and I was glad she was never there for the first few nights after you'd been away when the warmth of your body caused the steam to rise from the bedclothes and drift in the candle-light. One particularly rainy summer a spring opened up beneath the kitchen floor and I had to do the cooking ankle-deep in crystal water. We had a calor stove to cook on and in the winter I used to cook wearing my aunt's old fur coat because the window was so small I had to leave the door open so I could see what I was doing.

There was a gas light but its mantle kept crumbling and I couldn't be bothered with it. When there were men present they manned the Tilley lamps, but I never bothered with those either if I was the only adult there. I didn't like the idea of all that pressure, and anyway I never worked out the system of pushes and pauses. I stuck to oil lamps and candles, despite the danger of fire.

SHORTLY BEFORE WE arrived Dr Beeching had axed all the local railways, cunningly choosing his moment to coincide with a new interest in North Wales and a great increase in tourism, so that people who had them had to come by car. We hadn't got one so had to take the train to Ruabon where we were picked up by one Mr Jones, a gentleman from Bala. We relied on him, too, to bring us out our weekly provisions, and it was too bad if I forgot anything, for the walk to Bala and back embraced twelve miles. Sometimes in cases of real emergency – such as when I ran out of fags – we had to do it, thinking steadfastly of Mary Jones who in 1800 walked twenty-five miles barefoot to Bala from Llanfihangel-y-pennant to pick up her Bible from the Methodist preacher, Thomas Charles, thus somehow giving rise to the British and Foreign Bible Society.

There is a large stone standing on the hillside outside Bala bearing a brass plaque. When you leave the road and trudge up to it, knee-deep in sodden bracken, you find not that some ancient hero slew on this spot some ancient pest, but that here and in the field opposite were held the first sheepdog trials in 1873. While at first this revelation comes as something of an anticlimax, a moment's consideration reveals its true significance. Sheepdog trials play a large part in rural life and I used to find them some of the more enjoyable social occasions – as long as it didn't rain the *whole* time. It is much pleasanter watching a bunch of sheep being rounded up than staring at people running in a relay race or tearing round after a ball, and nobody sings Handel at sheepdog trials. They are relaxing for the observer and you can drink tea and eat cakes sitting on the grass. Occasionally a shepherd would appear too avid for victory and you would tremble for the fate of his dogs should they muff the round-up, but on the whole the atmosphere was unhurried and easy and you could watch the contest from a peace-inducing distance.

I never used to watch the prowess of a dog or shepherd I knew personally, just as I used to try and sneak out of the school eisteddfod when Mair or another of my more musical and talented friends rose on the stage to sing *penillion*, play the harp or piano, or recite some horrendous, endless poem. I just knew they'd fall off the edge, throttle themselves on an impossible high note or simply forget the whole thing. My fears were usually groundless but I never could shake them off and I still never watch a live performance of anything if I can avoid it – certainly never from the front row.

Sheep, of course, are always making fools of themselves. They seem to get more stupid and pusillanimous as they grow older and, whereas lambs manifest curiosity and trust, by the time they're a year old their behaviour and deportment as you approach remind you of housewives in a supermarket reputed to be on fire, or possibly at a Harrods china sale.

Rams are even stupider. They respond like the dumbest type of human male to an imagined slight or the idea that somebody might be muscling in on their territory, lowering their brows and bracing their shoulders. I once saw one taking offence at something in the demeanour of a stone wall. He charged it at about sixty miles an hour and broke his neck.

However, I like to see sheep quietly eating grass in a field as God intended: the traditional sort of Welsh sheep in a field of primeval untidiness, littered with ancient grey boulders and stunted, windswept thorns. That ancient, ancient greyness of rock and the dull, olive green of high fields is one of my most enduring and satisfying images. And the lambs chasing each other along a ridge in the blue spring evenings.

Earlier this month in an autumn evening I was walking back from the church when I saw a group of seven sheep posed around the bole of an old grey tree, its leaves just turning to gold. Some were standing, some lying, all watching me thoughtfully. The sun was just going down behind our hill and the shadow swept over them and they didn't move. I would have stayed and stared them out, but it grew cold.

In passing, we were always told that if we were threatened by a ram we should lie down immediately, thus disabling the creature from engaging his horns in your person. This doesn't work with bulls who, if prevented from goring, will jump up and down on you. If chased by a bull you have to keep running.

SOON AFTER WE took over Stacros I learned that in all Britain the area round Bala is the most prone to earthquake and seismic disturbance. Bloody marvellous. Indeed, only a few years ago, in our present house, I was sitting quietly alone one morning when an earthquake occurred. Nothing really shook, but there was a sound and a sensation as of vast earth-moving machinery: which I suppose it was in a way. It gave me a bit of a turn, but on examining my responses in a cooler moment I found I felt rather flattered. It isn't everyone, after all, who has sat through an earthquake.

Less gratifying – *much* less gratifying – is the radioactivity which has afflicted us since Chernobyl. I read only the other day that the count is still high in the area between Lake Bala and Lake Vyrnwy. That's where we are – precisely where we are – and while the authorities are extremly shifty about it the word is that all those sheep are still sending Geiger counters into cónvulsions. And what about the pheasants, I ask myself. Are they immune to radioactivity, or will the gentry, tucking into a modest *faisan en casserole* or a game pie find they have more than lead pellets to bargain with?

When you think of the natural disasters to which we are subject – not to mention the naturally occurring toxic substances in the locality (residual lead in some of the streams, radon build-up in the stone houses standing on stone) – you wonder what can possess the human race so to compound the dangers and inconveniences of existence. Are things not, you enquire, limp with exasperation, bad enough already?

Llyn Tegid – the lake of Bala – lies over an earlier town which, like so much of the Principality, was once subjected to inundation on account of the badness of its ruler. For a long time there were heard cries of '*Dial araw, dial araw!*' (Vengeance is coming) echoing dolefully in the night, but no one took any notice except for – yes, you've guessed it – the harpist who alone escaped to sit twanging his harp on the hillside, wringing out his robe and doubtless reflecting that justice had been done.

The word on the street is, and has been through the centuries, that Bala is in line for yet another flood; not this time, surely, because of malpractice on the part of the rulers. Those, I imagine, would now be the district councillors and I am certain that they are upright and well behaved. If it does happen again it will just be rotten luck and the harpist will not be justified in saying 'I told you so'.

ANOTHER STRETCH OF land is said to lie under what is now Cardigan Bay. According to one story Maes Gwyddno was flooded when a maiden who was in charge of a well failed to perform some hydraulic duty. Possibly she neglected to take the plug out at a crucial moment. It is difficult now to envisage the circumstances. A more popular version refers to Seithenyn who was in charge of the dykes. He got hopelessly drunk and let the sea in by forgetting to wield a particular lever.

Strange things happened in Welsh lakes. At Llyn yr Afanc on the Conwy there lived a horrible monster who greatly inconvenienced the local inhabitants, splashing around so much that he flooded the crops and drowned the cattle. Putting their heads together, they thought up a scheme to capture him: they would nominate a good-looking girl to sit by his pool and lure him out. Picture the scene as the girls made their excuses or prudently went to visit friends. Eventually a heroine was found to play the role of tethered goat and she sat herself down and waited. After a while out came the *afanc* and, so the tale relates, went to sleep with his head on her lap and a hand round her breast. (I think something may have been left out here. It is all most sinister.) Then along came the stout fellows of the village and bound him with chains, whereupon he awoke in a towering passion and flung himself back in the lake, tearing off the girl's breast in his haste. (We are not told whether she was rewarded with a pension, or possibly a medal for which there would now be ample room on her chest. Oh God.) This is a really nasty story. They grabbed the chains and fastened them to two renowned long-horned oxen who dragged him miles and miles to Llyn Ffynnon Las where they left him. On the way the eye of one of the oxen popped out and formed a pool – Pwll Llygad yr Ych – and, all in all, that is not a tale to tell to the kiddies on a winter's evening.

Tell them instead the story of the noble hound Gelert, the dog of Llewelyn. Llewelyn *may* have had a dog called Kill Hart. It says that he had in a MS dated 1692. I think his wife gave it to him, but it was killed by the horns of a hart while it was engaged in the chase – a kind of poetic justice. The story of Gelert appears in full first in Jones's *Musical Relicks of the Welsh Bards* in 1794. In 1800 Spencer wrote a poem about it, and then the local pub landlord constructed an actual grave in order to drum up trade.

The tale has at least the merit of poignancy, a brave and faithful hound and a stupid lord leaping to conclusions and killing it because he thinks it has eaten his baby when, in fact, it has killed the ravening wolf (though now I come to think of Rottweilers perhaps Llewelyn wasn't as utterly misguided as future generations have thought).

The original tale appears in Sanskrit some centuries BC with a thing called an ichneumon in the starring role. Left alone in the house with the baby while the mother went to the well, it slew a serpent approaching the cradle, and when the mother came back she saw the ichneumon with blood on its mouth and threw the bucket at it, so it died. The translators of this story didn't know what an ichneumon was and so described it variously as a dog or a cat or a weasel. I bet it was a mongoose.

I am gratified to know that George Borrow believed the story of Gelert, finding it very affecting. Since he was much given to swanking about his knowledge of other languages and cultures he might have known that versions of the Gelert legend appear all over Europe and the East.

I'd like to know what the then locals made of Borrow. He was over six foot, which is tall for a show-off since it is usually little men who talk too much in order to assert themselves, and he kept joining in other people's conversations, enlightening them from his lofty standpoint and asking silly questions, or congratulating himself, as he remarks in *Wild Wales*: 'I astonished the old man with my knowledge of Welsh and horses.'

When he visited Beaumaris he gazed out, as one does, over the bay to the 'noble rocky coast of the mainland – the most remarkable object of which is the gigantic Penmaen Mawr'. Here he began to talk to himself. '"What a bay!" said I, "for beauty it is superior to the far-famed one of Naples. A proper place for the keels to start from, which unguided by the compass found their way over the mighty and mysterious Western ocean!"' If he returned now he would doubtless find himself speechless to see the 'great head-stone' whittled away to a molehill and the Expressway adding an interesting note to the shoreline, but then he stood reciting 'all the Bardic lines I could remember connected with Madoc's expedition and likewise many from the Madoc of Southey . . .'

This is because he was thinking of the tradition which holds that Prince Madoc, who may or may not have been the son of Owain Gwynedd, discovered America in 1171. I think the story is that he set off, discovered America, came back and then set off again with a number of his subjects and, this time, he stayed. It is said that later visitors were surprised to be met by a tribe of Red Indians speaking fluent Welsh, but the tribe was destroyed by smallpox in the nineteenth century and now no evidence remains. Iolo Morgannwg, who was given to improving on the facts, did much in the eighteenth century to further the tale, but sadly it seems not to be true. Borrow was a remarkably gullible man.

HERE I MUST admit that a rationalist might accuse *me* of gullibility. For instance, I believe in ghosts and I am strongly inclined to believe in flying saucers. Lying in bed in Stacros on summer nights I was often conscious of – how can it be described? – a low hum, a reverberation, just below hearing so that the more you strained your ears the more elusive it became. Beyond the window lay the flat stretch of meadow, a remote and perfect spot for aliens to land, but they never did. Or if they did they didn't tell me.

I didn't even hear the Bang on the Berwyns, because I was away at the time. This Bang was heard for miles around, startling a community accustomed to affright and sudden noises from the RAF who persist in practising low-flying through the valleys. (This exercise is widely criticised as not merely disturbing the peace, but as grossly expensive and entirely futile, since millions of quids' worth of aeroplane hurtles around at about 250 feet above the ground, and to be effective in time of war it would have to fly at under 100 feet to escape radar surveillance. At this altitude the enemy could simply lasso it from the housetops, and anyway if things ever came to this pitch there really wouldn't be any point in anything any more. This is, of course, merely the view of the man in the lane, but it does not lack validity.)

Even the residents who were old enough to remember the quarrying never heard a Bang to match it. It never was explained.

There have been many sightings of strange things in West Wales. In 1977 a number of Pembrokeshire schoolchildren saw a UFO land and when, directed by their headmaster, they made drawings of the object, they produced remarkably similar representations. I could go on about the circumstantial evidence here, but those who are prepared to believe me will believe me already, and those who are not would not believe me if a flying saucer landed on their hat. So I will merely say that there are several published accounts of these happenings, and recommend a trip to the library. UFOs have been spotted from Snowdon to Cardiff and a few people have encountered spacemen – some gigantic, some fishy-looking and all disconcerting. One feature of the closer encounters is that when earthlings are invited into spaceships they tend to lose all sense of time; not because they are enjoying themselves so hugely, but because time seems to become irrelevant.

This was a feature of the experiences of those who went away with the Tylwyth Teg – the Rip Van Winkle syndrome. The Fairy Folk used to dance in circles, and if a human being, beguiled by the sweetness of their music, stepped in to join them he was lost, unless somebody had the presence of mind to fetch him out by throwing him one end of a rowan branch and hauling on the other. Some people disappeared for ever and some returned after days or maybe years, thinking that they had been gone for only a few minutes.

In one case a man who imagined himself to be about twenty-five thought he had merely dropped off for a snooze and, on waking, stretching himself and yawning, went back home for his tea. There he was met by an old man he'd never seen before and, after an exchange distinguished by mutual misunderstanding, it turned out that the party of the second part was the nephew of the party of the first part.

After some time and much explanation the nephew, moved by family feeling, stepped forward to embrace his uncle who promptly crumbled away into dust. I am sure we all have relations we would not be overjoyed to see standing on our doorstep, but ask yourself what your reaction would be if they came to pieces in your hands.

The Ceffyl Dŵr too, when he maintained his equine persona and wasn't turning himself into a frog, used to take people for rides out of time, and men have entered the mountain halls never to be seen again. There may be many mundane reasons for these disappearances – insanity, strong drink, and simple misfortune as well as the need for a Good Excuse: 'Late for dinner? Surely not, *cariad*. I was only in that fairy ring five minutes . . .' – but I prefer the more esoteric explanations.

APART FROM THE hum Stacros was remarkably free of psychic manifestations. One visitor noticed that all the birds took to the forest, and the other shy, wild creatures took to the hills when I arrived with the children, so perhaps the ghosts and the fairies also made themselves scarce as they saw Mr Jones approaching with a carload. Sometimes in the summer noon I would feel a sense of oppression when the shadows lay at odd angles and the sunlight held a quality of blackness, but as it was usually raining I didn't suffer too greatly from the noon-day devil. When it was fine I sat on the slope reading, or with the little ones down by the stream as they dammed it. The older children were usually employed tracking each other through the trees or, I am afraid, taking potshots at the few unwary trippers who came our way. It was a perfect place for children.

I did the washing by treading on it in the bath and rinsing it in the stream, and since we had no fridge and no means of getting to the shop frequently, cooking was largely a matter of boiling potatoes and pasta and opening tins.

Spam curry was my *pièce de résistance*. I kept as much fruit as possible before it rotted – 'No, child, that banana isn't bad. It's black because it grew that way' – but we had no means of storing fresh meat, even if we could have afforded it, and green vegetables lose their virtue soon after they're picked. I used sometimes to fear the onset of scurvy, although in season I made sorrel and dandelion salads and nettle soup.

Sometimes when my mother or one of my aunts came to stay they would reminisce about a childhood treat which consisted of chopped dock leaves fried with oatmeal in bacon fat, but for some reason they never offered to make it for us. I think it was one of those memories best left nostalgically undisturbed. Dock leaves, as far as I'm concerned, were put there by a merciful Providence to minister to nettle stings,

although if you used, say, spinach and didn't go mad with the bacon fat I can see that this dish could be rather good.

What they did do was to make Welsh cakes, *crempogau*, potato cakes and a kind of soda bread on the griddling iron over the open fire. I never did manage to achieve the perfection which seemed to come naturally to the Griffiths girls, and can only assume that this is one of those skills which has to be acquired in childhood. Since, as a child, I had thought of cooking as a sissy business all was lost.

My aunt Maggi would never put butter *and* jam on the same piece of bread, considering this to be disgustingly decadent, extravagant and luxurious, and all of them ate their porridge with salt, not sugar. An ancient Welsh dish was called *llymru* and was made by steeping oatmeal in water for a couple of nights, and then straining off the liquid, boiling and stirring it until it thickened. It was eaten with milk and salt, so I suppose my aunts were adhering in some way to the customs of their childhood.

They made very good stews and broths too, but their roast meat always turned out tough, and they had the appalling habit of putting a lump of bicarbonate of soda in the water when they boiled (and boiled and boiled) any green vegetables. This certainly kept them green, but it made them taste like very old and much-used dish cloths. The other thing they made perfectly was crisp treacle toffee. Mine usually has the consistency of Tarmacadam pavements in a very hot summer.

It was easier when the bilberries and raspberries were out. Wild raspberries grew in a dry ditch and I spent hours picking them. I spent even longer picking off the maggots when I got them home. I'd sprinkle the raspberries with sugar, which the maggots obviously hated, for they would struggle up for air and I'd clobber the little bastards with a matchstick as soon as they emerged.

There were tiny wild pansies in the field, St John's Wort and forget-me-nots in the soggier areas and wild cresses in the stream. Regretfully we never gathered these for fear of the dreaded liver fluke – a nasty thing which starts off in sheep and can end up in human beings if they're not careful. Later in the year grew foxgloves and rose-bay willow herb and I'd put jam jars full of them in all the rooms of the cottage. In a sense I played house, for the place was so simple and so sparsely furnished it was more like a child's plaything than a proper habitation – apart from the fact that the work one did have to do was back-breaking.

I think Stacros may have stood on one of the old pilgrim ways in the days when Wales was full of saints and people went from shrine to shrine – some of them to ask for favours, but some to pray. One Easter I wrote a poem which I've lost. I wrote it because from Good Friday to Easter Sunday, when Our Lord was gone from us, the skies were low, and as heavy and grey as pewter, while all around the meadow grass was shimmering gold. For those three days the earth held more light than the sky. There was a holiness about Stacros.

IN A WAY winter posed fewer problems. For one thing it was so cold that the turkey could sit frozen in the pantry for weeks. There were frost patterns on the bedroom windows and I had to exercise ingenuity to stop the pipes from freezing up, but thick snow meant I could take the baby out in a basket roped to a sledge, which was easier on both of us since the paths around were not designed for pushchairs. There is something extraordinary about the hills in snow; something magical and theatrical yet true like a solemn High Mass with white vestments, but you need to be alone to appreciate it. Skiers and winter sports enthusiasts quite spoil the atmosphere. A mountainside under snow is a holy thing. Even the forest was lovely if you went to the edges where icicles hung from the low branches and the snow had been blown by the wind into hollows and harbours for darkness.

The worst times came as night fell and the children weren't home. The only words I have ever really feared are, 'The children aren't home.' I would go round the paths and the woods carrying the baby and calling; but they always came back then – dripping, dishevelled and tattered, with bits of twig in their jumpers and holes in the seats of their pants. The fire would be high and bright, the candles glowing and the soup simmering one-sidedly on the range. I'd finally get them all to bed and sit alone and read till the fire died. I love a house full of sweetly sleeping children.

Sometimes, of course, we had visitors. Anyone with the merest hovel, if it is situated in the country, always has visitors. They wake up one morning, look out over the dustbins and the high-rise blocks of town and they say to themselves, 'Let's go and see so-and-so in the country.' I didn't really mind, and some of them were positively welcome, for they came in motorcars, thus alleviating the constant nagging anxiety that one might run out of cigarettes and have to walk to Bala. The farmer from Maesafallan used to leave a can of milk at the bottom of the path every morning, but as it was at least a mile from cottage to milk-dropping-off point, it was easier to wake a sleeping guest and make him drive down to get it than to bully or bribe the children, or go and get it myself.

The path was known as the Milk Path and bordered a smallish ravine down which the stream ran and somersaulted and sometimes rested in a deep pool.

The brave, the warm-blooded used to swim in this pool, and one day a man who had come to put the slates back on the roof threw three weeks' worth of accumulated garbage in it. I had asked him to take it to the municipal dump, but he couldn't be bothered. Organic waste I dropped over the forest fence for the rabbits, weasels, foxes, feral cats, worms, beetles, hedgehogs, mice, etc.; waste paper and cardboard I burned on the range; but apart from digging great holes in the field there was nothing I could do with the numerous tins and bottles but ask people to take them away to the place appointed for them. I spent weeks after that retrieving shaming bits of detritus from miles of stream.

The rowans grew out over the abyss and I made the more agile children crawl along the swaying branches to pick clusters of berries so I could make rowan jelly. I used to make buckets of it. And elderflower and crab apple, and damson, and raspberry and bilberry. I don't any more.

I think we never recognise the best days for what they are, since at the time they are not perfect. Nothing in life is *quite* perfect, and I used often to think of how tired I was and how easy it would be when the children were grown up. Now I sometimes wish I had died one quiet silver night when they were all asleep and I could hear only the stream and the wind in the forest. But the poor little creatures would have had a very

great shock to find Mama expired with a cheerful smile on her face, and no breakfast ready. They would have had to walk to Bala to explain, and might perhaps still stand in need of psychiatric help. One mustn't be selfish.

One morning I went down to the stream for water (I suppose the cows had trodden on the pipe again so there was none coming through the taps) and I saw a feral cat alone in the meadow. He was stroking his chin against the grasses, his eyes half closed, holding his tail high: perfectly solitary, unselfconscious and glad in the warm morning. I have seen many happy cats, but they are usually sitting purring on a cushion or

somebody's knee, or drinking milk. I have never seen anything evincing such high pride and joy as that lone tom in the meadow grass. When he caught sight of me all his gladness went and he flew off into the forest.

Some summers there were so many feral kittens about that I scarcely dared go out, especially when my daughter was small. They would sit in the hedgerows waiting for her and scream piteously as she drew near – 'Mama, Mama' – and we'd find ourselves with yet another cat.

THE MOST AWKWARD days were when the stream was in spate after much rain. Normally placid, chuckling and easy-going, it would undergo a total character change, and you would wake early to look out and see it roaring and seething, grey and foaming with rage, beyond all reason or appeal.

Broken boughs, clumps of reeds, corpses of little animals, and indeed of larger ones such as sheep, would be swept across the meadow and down the *cwm*, and the wooden bridge which usually bestrode it would lie beneath it. The bridge had not given the impression of complete reliability for some years. Drivers would always get out of their cars and examine its planks and piles closely before deciding whether to risk it or to drive through the stream, but when the floods came they either had to give up and go back or go the long way round – up towards Vyrnwy and down again through the forest.

The noble postman never failed. My friends and relations were under instructions to write frequently, for as I had no other means of communication I could always prevail on the Royal Mail to drop in a shopping list at Mr Jones's and a request that he come out a.s.a.p. I was pretty smart at improvisation – I once made rather good bread using a quarter of a can of warm bitter as a raising agent – but no food at all poses real problems. The children would volunteer to shoot the rapids but I forbade it.

Oddly enough, apart from this major inconvenience I don't remember being much discommoded by the rain. It never seemed to stop the children from going out to play

in the long grass and the sodden woods. There were always wet clothes draped in front of the range, or over the bubbling cistern, for even when they weren't being rained on they were falling in the stream, but I must have just got used to it. Rows and rows of steaming, up-ended wellies were part of our lives.

One day I lit the fire and put a bare foot into a wellington boot preparatory to going to the shed for some coal. In the boot already was a large black beetle. As I was

regaining my composure, the fourth son fell over the banister and split his forehead open, and the chimney caught fire. By the purest chance there were two foresters high on the hill behind the cottage. They coped with the chimney and put a butterfly plaster on the baby's wound. I had myself already coped with the black beetle by dint of shaking it out and treading on it with the other welly. It was then decided that the baby's wound should be stitched and they drove us into Bala to the doctor's surgery. We had spent weeks up there without seeing another living soul – apart from the matutinal postman – so while the whole episode was unfortunate it also gave evidence of a benign providence. I still wonder what I'd have done if they hadn't been there. I might have razed the forest to the ground while the baby bled to death. If the situation had been less fraught the mere presence of the beetle might have sent me into hysterics. It is surprising the resources one can call upon in a real emergency.

I HAVE SO far neglected to mention that I often had not only my own five sons but the sons of several other people as well, so that sometimes there would be as many as eight, nine or ten hungry, adventurous and soaking children roaming the countryside in search of further diversion. There was the night they all sneaked out and started up the bulldozer – but I never got to the bottom of that story. I didn't really want to and, on reflection, I find I still don't. There were other occasions too . . . but best to let sleeping dogs lie.

One of the more sensible things I ever did was to collar Alfie. When he was seven he, and about a hundred of his friends, broke into our house in London under the justifiable impression that it was a derelict building. They all got away except for Alfie and he never has. He started coming to Wales with us then also, fell hopelessly in love with the place and has every intention of bringing his bones to rest here in the graveyard. He was the youngest of ten and therefore used to the exigencies of family life. He was also, always, amazingly competent, and although he was only a few years older than my eldest son he was helpful: *really* consistently helpful, most of the time.

Alfie had his lapses. There was the day they decided to train George, the forest horse whose job it was to haul logs, as a riding steed. They chased him round the field for hours, got on and fell off, and it's a miracle they weren't trampled to death. George was a nice horse but there are limits.

Then there was the time Alfie fell out with the farmer's wife, who until then had been his dearest friend. I believe he dropped water bombs on her campers who ran to her to complain, but again I'm not sure of the details.

You may ask why I was not more alert at the time, but in all probability I was engaged in making sandwiches – Mother's Pride, marg, pilchards, corned beef, salmon and shrimp paste, egg and slices of onion, tomato, and cucumber for the vitamin content. I would have been trying to remember who didn't like what with what and wondering whether there was enough to go round. The children could have woken Arthur and his Knights in their fastness before I'd made enough sandwiches. They all also had the large innocent eyes of childhood and were perfect little liars. Just as well really. If I'd known what they were up to I'd have spent the whole time sitting in judgment and nobody would have had any fun at all. Least of all me.

It was Alfie who mended the upstairs window by standing outside on a box on a chair on another box on a table while I stood inside, helping. And it was me who said, 'Darling, hang on. I'll run down and catch you', when the edifice started to sway. This must have happened about twenty years ago and Alfie has never got over the idiocy of my remark. As he says, by the time I'd shot down the stairs, he'd have been sitting in a pile of matchwood.

It was Alfie who was in the kitchen one day being me and peeling carrots (I don't know where I was) when George got stuck in the doorway. The kitchen suddenly darkened and Alfie thought 'It's going to rain', but when he looked at the window he saw blue sky. He tells me it took a lot of thought, ingenuity and persuasion to get George back to where he was supposed to be.

It was Alfie who frightened me nearly to death by running home and saying he'd seen a murderer lurking in the trees beyond the bridge. This timeless and universal threat afflicts all women alone with the children in the wilderness. 'Bar the doors, pass me the poker, if he comes through this window jump out of that one!' I thought at the time that Alfie had probably only seen a forester looking at trees or a shepherd looking for sheep – but you never *know*. We had very few unexpected callers there, although there was once a large party of lost Youth Hostellers who had to be revived with pilchard and corned-beef sandwiches before they could proceed.

Once upon a time nobody locked their doors. Callers would walk in and say, 'Is the woman of the house at home?' There were murders, certainly, but usually of the domestic type, which, while they shock society, do not arouse the terror and revulsion inspired by the unknown marauder. Everyone can, to some extent, sympathise with

the irritation which leads a person to lay violent hands on his nearest and dearest, but the unknown assassin is an outlaw, a wolf and greatly to be feared. He was rare in the hills and valleys where strangers seldom ventured – save for those clad in shorts and bearing knapsack, Thermos and map, whose worst crime was leaving the gate open.

Our predecessor at Stacros, the Oxford don, once forgot to throw a bottle of sherry into his car boot, and it was still on the doorstep when he went back three months later. Now with 'improved communications', i.e. roads everywhere, there is no telling what riff-raff may be abroad on the hillsides. A man with a van once called to ask if we had any old junk we wanted to get rid of. By this he meant had we got any irreplaceable Welsh oak dressers, chests, settles, etc. Quick as a flash I told him in a houseproud tone of voice that I didn't entertain any old rubbish and bought everything brand new in bits from a place on the North Circular Road in London, and he went away wearing a disconsolate air.

In the last century a girl was murdered at a farm near Penrhyndeudraeth – absolutely chopped to pieces – by a similar sort of man on the same quest for valuable trifles. He was called Thomas Edwards and they hanged him at Dolgellau in 1813. Serve him right.

An old woman once called at Stacros and said that she used to go there as a child to help her auntie, the shepherd's wife. She remembered washing lettuce in the stream for tea for the men who had come to help with the sheep shearing. Apart from the conifers, she said, little had changed. It has now. I've heard. I can't go back and see. My heart would break. She was a staunch old lady to go back through the courses of her past. I can't even look at old photographs. I only remember that the days at Stacros were magical. I've forgotten the sleepless nights, the work, the lack of money and comfort. All I remember is that *they* were the happiest days of my life and they've gone.

If I'd been asked then if I was happy I'd have said I hadn't got the time to think about it. I was too busy washing nappies, making dinner, and advising the current baby not to put his fingers in the sheepdog's eyes. Anyway, I'd have said loftily that happiness is a by-product and not to be sought after. I often said that and I still believe it, but I wish we knew enough to appreciate happiness when we've got it.

THE LEASE ON Stacros ran out. We went round and round looking for another house that would feel the same. We looked at dozens of them. I didn't want to leave the district, for when I think of home I think of here. London is merely somewhere I live when I'm not at home, and it would have been pointless to go and live in further exile somewhere else.

After a while we found this house. It hadn't been lived in for forty years. The floorboards had rotted away, the roof had fallen in and bats hung on what was left of the rafters. Through the middle of the house ran a small river. 'That's it,' we said to each other, 'that's the one.' A door opened from what had been a hayloft on to the mountainside, and on that door somebody had written: 'It does not matter who I am, for this must surely be a part of Heaven. Just stand here and really listen.'

The house lies in a valley underneath a cliff where ravens and buzzards nest. It has the remains of a cruck, which takes it back many centuries, and the walls are about three feet thick. It is a long house, which means that whenever the inhabitants thought they needed more space they added another room on to the end. The last one went up in Victorian times – you can tell simply by the feel of it. There is a partition of oak, which has the air of Tudor, which kept the animals apart from the people, and what used to be the dairy is now the back kitchen. There was a bread-oven when we came, but the stone had fallen and rotted and it had to go. The small river had to go too and the bats went of their own accord. (They are still around, in case anyone is worried about them.) A family of redstarts lives in the walls and swallows nest under the barn eaves. Rabbits live in the *tŷ bach* – the old outside lavatory – and sheep live in what would be the garden if I had green fingers. I don't want to make a garden, for gardens are too subject to change, reminding you as seasons pass that time is flowing away. I prefer to keep the grass and the camomile and the harebells, not to mention the thistles and the nettles. These things have their own time and their own purpose and exist, reassuringly, without our interference.

We were living here when our second son, Joshua, died, and his death formed a hinge in existence. Everything that had happened before led up to it, and everything that has happened since is only afterwards. He lies in the graveyard across the fields and

one day I shall lie beside him and it won't matter any more. I do not know how people contain such pain. His father wrote this epitaph for him:

JOSHUA HAYCRAFT
who died 21 May 1978
aged nineteen years
after a fall

IOSVE
CVI · PRÆCIPITI · DECIDENTI
NON · STETIT · SOL
SED · PRÆCEPS · OCCIDIT
SOLIBVS · REDEVNTIBVS
IPSE · REDITVRVS
IN · NOMINE · IESV
NOMINE · TVO
CARISSIME · DVLCISSIME
RESVRGES

Joshua,
for whom the sun
did not stand still,
but as you fell headlong
so set for you,
as suns return
you too, most sweet beloved,
will return
and in the name of him
whose name is yours
rise again

David Gentleman designed the sun emblem specifically for Joshua and later I found some seventeenth- and eighteenth-century tombstones bearing precisely the same emblem, which was oddly comforting.

Curiously enough, another consolation is the enemy, time. As it takes my son further away from me, it brings me closer to him. Our daughter, who was born when our youngest son was five, dreamed one night that she had died and was met at the gates of Heaven by my first daughter, who had only lived for two days. In Heaven she had grown up and was the age that she would have been in time. She led her sister to Our Lady who picked her up in her great hand and prepared her for Heaven, and there she saw her brother 'even handsomer than he had been in life'. She saw other dead relations and all Heaven was the colour of Our Lady, the colour of the brightest snow. There was a vast table laden with fruit, and she had a sense of love such as she had never known, feeling God as a Presence. This too is a consolation, for I believe in her vision. Gerald of Wales observes somewhere that dreams are like rumours. Some can be readily discounted while others are true and must be believed – like Homer's dreams of ivory and horn.

There is a space at the front of the house where there used to be an orchard. Once I vowed that, in the future, I would replant it; but the future has somehow gone – the future that I had expected – and I only have the present. There seems no compelling reason to do anything very much in the present, so unless somebody else takes over the project the apple and the plum in blossom will remain a memory. You may ask, 'But what about the next generation?' To which I respond that the next generation can plant its own fruit trees. We have to leave it something to do.

THE PLACE ON earth where I come closest to peace is in the graveyard amongst all the quiet dead. I seem to have thought, all my life, of little but death – partly perhaps because of impatience, a yearning to have it over and done with: that extraordinary last thing that we are called upon to do, the act of dying. If we have to do it – I think to myself – I would rather do it sooner than later. But mostly it comes from the old awareness that I am not whole, that there is something missing: something more important than all the world. Death is the price we must pay for completion. I am astonished when I think that two of my children have achieved this feat and I am left here, not knowing what they know. Simple curiosity is another strong element in this possibly lamentable death wish.

There is a harpist lying in the graveyard whose epitaph reads: 'The singer is silent, but not the song.' Another epitaph, roughly translated, reads: 'Lord, why did you make the valley so beautiful, and the life of the poor shepherd so short?' Poetry is another consolation, but sometimes I think that in all this peaceful land there is not one spot that has not, at one time or another, been soaked in blood and the tears of the bereaved and dispossessed.

The church is dedicated to St Monacella – in Welsh, Melangell. In some accounts she is described as the daughter of an Irish king who tried to force her into an unwelcome marriage, whereupon she fled across the sea until she came to this valley. Others say she was a descendant of Macsen Wledig (Magnus Maximus, a Spaniard who made himself Emperor of Rome and whose story is told in the Mabinogion). All are agreed, however, upon what happened next. She lived for fifteen years on a sheltered ledge at the back of our house (which at that time wasn't there, you understand) until one day Brochwel Ysgythrog, the Prince of Powys, came charging along in pursuit of a hare. The hare, seeing Melangell sitting there, leaped for protection under the folds of her robe, and the Prince and his huntsman stood, feeling somewhat at a loss.

Now the story has been a little embroidered. The huntsman, raising his horn to blow it, found it was stuck to his face, which must have been mightily inconvenient, and the hounds fled, howling. Brochwel was so impressed that he gave her some lands and the privilege of sanctuary to all who fled thither for protection. Other women now came to join her and she established a convent.

She lived there another thirty-seven years, working miracles for those who sought her favour. After her death a certain Elisse came to Pennant intending to violate the community. The records state tersely that he died there 'in a most dreadful manner'.

The infuriating brevity of this leaves the mind boggling. There certainly was an Elisse at that date. In the *Annales Cambriae* of 814 it is recorded that one Griffydd ap Cyngan of Powys was treacherously murdered by his brother Elisse, who was clearly a very bad man and not to be regretted.

A much sadder story is that of Iorwerth Drwyndwn, the eldest son of Owain Gwynedd, Prince of North Wales, who because of the size and shape of his nose was detested by everybody and deprived of the succession. He fled over the hills to Pennant for sanctuary when his brother, Dafydd, ascended the throne, but he must have foolishly ventured out one day, for he was killed at a place called Bwlchgroes Iorwerth, not very far away. His effigy lies with that of Melangell in the church. In the eighteenth century the then vicar iconoclastically laid about this effigy with a hatchet, but it still survives. There is also a huge bone in the church, known as the Giant's Rib, described in one publication as 'probably the bone of some fish'. It was found on the mountain between Bala and Pennant and God alone knows how it got there.

In passing, Christianity came to Wales in the third century in the form of monasticism. This was not the rule of St Benedict but the Egyptian type of monasticism favoured by the desert Fathers. Many holy men and women lived alone in cells as anchorites or hermits, largely independent, but ruled over by an abbot. Later on came Benedictines, Cistercians, Dominicans and Franciscans. There were monasteries all over the place – often as much engaged in farming as in preaching the word.

HERE, WHERE ONCE the convent may have stood, was a farm until, in all likelihood because of the system of gavelkind whereby estates were shared out equally amongst relations, the acreage was diminished until it was no longer workable. The barns were in use until fairly recently and were therefore in a better state than was the house. They are all haunted, and so is the land.

One night, some years ago, my friend Janet and I were sitting peacefully by the fire when another guest who had been watching moths behind the house (he hung a sheet over the washing line, put a lantern beside it and counted the moths who came from everywhere to fly around the light) came in and said that something was breathing out there. 'Stuff and nonsense,' we said, but were eventually prevailed upon to go out and listen.

Something was indeed breathing out there. Very loud and regular breathing. It sounded as though someone drunk had fallen asleep in a ditch at our feet, but there was no one there. We hunted and hunted and there was no one there. 'It's Elisse,' said somebody sagaciously, but the untroubled breathing was not that of a rapist and murderer, murdered in his turn. It was too peaceful, and I didn't find it frightening, just *so* odd.

The next night we had to dinner a number of people including Celia, our sub-postmistress and her husband, Alan, and Linda Mary, who is a deacon of the Church of England. As the last of the apple crumble disappeared I said, 'I wonder if the breathing is still going on?' I went out to listen and it was. Everyone came out to listen. Ten of us (including the children who are really no less reliable as witnesses than other people) fanned out over hundreds of yards, up the hill, down the meadow, and everyone, wherever he was, cried, 'It's getting louder up [or down] here', and the rest of us cried, 'It can't be. It's getting louder here.' I still didn't find it frightening, but then I was standing under the house wall with the door open behind me. Those up on the hill, away from the light, experienced that lifting of the hair on the back of the neck which signals the presence of the untoward. It wasn't the wind and it wasn't the water and it wasn't hedgehogs. I don't suppose I shall ever know what it was.

Some nights there is a loud, steady, rhythmic knocking from one of the barns. Alfie once lay awake for two hours, listening to it. Why, I asked, did he not go across to investigate? He scarcely bothered to answer me. We've heard it by day too, but found no explanation. I have heard voices in the night and once got out of bed to make certain I hadn't left the radio on. I couldn't find the light switch and then I remembered with certainty that I *had* turned the radio off – so I got back into bed. After all, there was little could do about it if the entire place was thronged with phantoms.

I have never felt that they were unhappy or hostile, not lost souls seeking satisfaction or vengeance, just lingering shadows and echoes of lives that once were here. Since the princes settled down or died out, abandoning their habits of rapine, pillage and bloodshed, nothing really dreadful has happened in the valley. Not as far as I know, that is, and I know of only one exception. An old man told me of a previous owner who had ridden, one evening, into the village. The horse, he said, came back, but not the rider. Good Heavens, said I, what had happened? The rider, said my informant, had been found floating face down in the river in suspicious circumstances, for there had been some dispute with the neighbours about a little matter of sheep-rustling. When was that, I asked, for he told it as though it had happened yesterday. The old man shrugged and said he didn't really know. He had had the story from his grandmother who had not been too hot on dates.

NEARBY, JUST OUTSIDE Llanrhaeadr-ym-Mochnant, where the waterfall is one of the Seven Wonders of Wales, a tall stone pillar stands in a field. Now, if we are to believe the old tales, the Welsh once suffered from dragons as other peoples have suffered from the moth. Some of them were large and terrible – I suppose they were the ones who had evolved from vipers, and a number of them lived round Penmaenmawr – and some, described in more recent accounts, were small and beautiful with bright wings. I think these were probably dragonflies, magnified by the effects of alcohol on the witness into something more threatening, but the dragon which harassed the people of Llanrhaeadr was not of this kind. It ate the animals and some of the inhabitants, until they hit on the idea of draping the pillar in red cloth, which colour, it seems, dragons particularly dislike. Seeing this horrid scarlet object, the dragon flew at it, thoughtless with rage, and beat and beat at it until it killed itself. I thought this cunning device charmingly trouble-free and economical of human life. Why didn't St George think of that?

I have just discovered the probable reason why dragons didn't care for the colour red. Until some time in the seventeenth century there was preserved in a castle in

Normandy a *red* velvet buckler, together with the shield and dagger which St Michael employed in his battle with the dragon. One wonders what the Red Dragon of Wales thought about actually being that shade. It must have been irritating for him.

It was at Llanrhaeadr ym Mochnant that Bishop William Morgan translated the Bible into Welsh, thereby preserving the language from fragmenting into innumerable local dialects or disappearing completely. Whenever I feel overwhelmed by the pressures – not of work, but of outside distractions and the turmoil of life – I remind myself of the Bishop who had a peculiar ability to get on the wrong side of people, thus involving himself in endless tiresome disputes and litigation, ending up in the Star Chamber. It seems remarkable that the Bishop managed to translate so much as a shopping list given what he had to contend with – family feuds, lawsuits, the disposition of livings and money problems. It is even said that he stood in his pulpit with a pistol at the ready in case the parishioners turned nasty. Perhaps he was one of those scholars who cannot cope with the world outside books. There are many such. It must also be admitted that the Welsh have a long, long history of feuding.

The Plough Inn which stands on the right as you come down the hill into Llanrhaeadr is a survival from earlier times and undoubtedly doomed. The beer is kept in barrels below stairs and the proprietor, Miss Edwards, goes down those stairs and brings back two glasses at a time. It is a wonderfully leisurely pub with no flashing lights or music and we can be sure that sooner or later somebody will come along and modernise it, and life will never be the same again. It used vaguely to remind me of a convent, simply – I hasten to assure you – because some convents have the same feeling of tradition and changelessness. But people cannot leave well enough alone and will tinker and fiddle, putting down carpet-tiles and arranging potted plants in the bend of the stairs. Some element in British life appears fixedly determined to cause everywhere and everything – churches, pubs, town centres, hotels, banks, railway stations – to resemble as closely as possible a suburban sitting-room, a *lounge*.

One of the churches used to have on its ceiling a map of the stars of heaven, painted by one of its vicars. Then another vicar came along and had it painted over. A great many vicars have this tendency to iconoclasm; theology seems to have an unfortunate

effect on the simple-minded, and vicars who, one feels, should know better, are still wreaking havoc with many places of 'worship', putting in lavatories and coffee bars and tearing out pews to make space for people to dance in. Oh well, I don't know which to mind most about – the churches or the pubs. (I must add that our present local vicar is untypical in that he is both erudite and charming, and appears to believe in God.)

It is all very depressing, but then I am easily depressed. Coming of Celtic and Russo-Finnish stock I suppose it could not be otherwise. Both these peoples are given to abrupt changes of mood, but are seldom merry for long, feeling more natural in a state of melancholy. I once read about some Finns, living on the edge of the Arctic Circle, who never drew a sober breath and all died before they were forty; concerned authority, in the effort to prolong their lives, put a prohibition on alcohol, so then they all died of cancer before they were forty. The Welsh are not as hell-bent on death as this, but they have always thought about it a good deal from the oldest times. They are seldom maudlin but frequently a little morbid.

IN THE EIGHTEENTH century, Sir John Pryce of Newtown took the cult of death to rather extreme lengths. His first two wives having expired, he married a third, who not surprisingly refused to get into the nuptial bed, taking exception to the fact that her two predecessors were lying, embalmed, on each side of it. She insisted on having them decently buried 'before she would supply their vocation', and I cannot find it in my heart to blame her.

He was not a tactful man, Sir John. When his second wife passed away he wrote to the curate of Newtown, the Rev. W. Felton, who was also dying: 'I have abundant reason to believe that you will immediately enter upon a happier state when you make an exchange, and I desire that you will do me the favour to acquaint my two dear Wives that I retain the same tender Affections and the same Honour and Esteem for their Memories which I ever did for their persons.' He went on to request that the Rev. Felton should bother God for the 'Divine permission' to let his second wife come back

and tell him who had 'wronged' her, thus causing her death, so that he could wreak vengeance on them. He reminds me of those irritating people who, when they hear you are going abroad, ask you to take two suitcases of luggage to their aunt who lives near your destination. Few people when about to travel wish to be further encumbered.

However, I think Sir John was uxorious to the point where he became unbalanced. When his third wife died he wrote to Bridget Bostock, the 'Cheshire Pythoness', who claimed to heal people with her 'fasting spittle' (supplied in corked bottles), asking if she could arrange to resuscitate her: 'I entreat you for God Almighty's sake that you would be so good as to come here, if your actual presence is absolutely requisite, to raise up my dear wife, Dame Eleanor Pryce, from the Dead.' It didn't work. I am also curious to know what the second Dame died of and why Sir John suspected foul play, but of course history does not relate. This is the maddening thing about so much history. (He was about to marry a fourth wife when he died himself.)

B UT ENOUGH OF all this talk of death. We all have to do time, and it is both unwise and ungrateful to yearn only for eternity. The *deryn y meirw* hammers at all our windows, whether we hear him or not, and whatever we make of his importunity. The old man who laid our fences had a heart attack, and when he recovered he said, '*Melys y bywyd*', which means life is sweet. I didn't understand him at the time and I still don't. I think that life is saccharine – a substitute, a shadow of the real thing. I believe Plato thought along similar lines but was able to express himself with more eloquence.

Even as I sit by the stream under the shade of the hawthorn, hand on the sun-warmed rock, watching the bees and the beetles and the birds doing concentratedly what they were conceived to do, feeling the grasses under my feet, and painstakingly identifying the wild flowers, I still cannot accept the moment for what it is. I know it will pass. Self-consciousness is the price we pay for the hope of immortality, and it is a

high price. You put your hand in the stream and it runs through your fingers. You pick the flowers and they die. You hear the birds of this year but they are not the birds of last year, and next year they will be different birds. You know that – pesticides and herbicides permitting – the genus will continue, but you also know that your own awareness will have changed, and that you will not be there. And the grief is not for your *self*, but that all the loveliness may go unseen and unrecorded, and no one will ever know how, for you, the blossom smelled, and the grasses bent, and the light changed – and how you got up to go home as the shadows fell and the air grew cold and you came back to another mode of existence: the habitations of men and the demands of life and the world.

It is perhaps easier to be sedated, to be bored, for at each moment of joyful consciousness comes the knowledge that it will pass; and as time passes, you realise it will never come again. It is more than that. It is an awareness that some of this world is so beautiful that it cannot be described; and, greedy and grasping as we are, we want not only to enjoy it but to tell it – so that it listens, and in listening becomes fixed – how unknowingly lovely it is. We look for a response from that which is unresponsive – for it takes no account of us. No wonder we dream of death, of a true consummation where longing ceases and the earth itself embraces us until we cannot be told apart, cannot be discerned, and have no more responsibility. This, perhaps, is why we dream of Heaven; this perhaps is what is meant by *hiraeth*: a lifelong yearning for what is gone or out of reach.

Captions and Index